The Architect's Guide
to Preventing Water Infiltration

Copyright © 2010 by John Wiley & Sons, Inc. All rights reserved.

Published by John Wiley & Sons, Inc., Hoboken, New Jersey

Published simultaneously in Canada

For general information about our other products and services, please contact our Customer Care Department within the United States at (800) 762-2974, outside the United States at (317) 572-3993 or fax (317) 572-4002.

Wiley also publishes its books in a variety of electronic formats. Some content that appears in print may not be available in electronic books. For more information about Wiley products, visit our web site at www.wiley.com.

Library of Congress Cataloging-in-Publication Data:

The architect's guide to prevent water infiltration / by Elmer Botsai . . . [et al.].
    p.   cm.
  Includes bibliographical references and index.
  ISBN 978-0-470-40165-1 (cloth)
  1. Waterproofing.   2. Dampness in buildings.   I. Botsai, Elmer E.
  TH9031.A73 2010
  693.8'92—dc22   2009033997

Printed in the United States of America

10 9 8 7 6 5 4 3 2 1

The Architect's Guide
to Preventing Water Infiltration

Elmer Botsai, ArchD, FAIA
Charles Kaneshiro, AIA, LEED-AP
Phil Cuccia, CSI, CDT
Hiram Pajo, AIA

WILEY

John Wiley & Sons, Inc.

Contents

Preface

My first meaningful encounter with Elmer Botsai was in 1992. He was the immediate past dean of the School of Architecture at the University of Hawaii, and I was a fourth-year student in the program. Elmer was leading a design crit of my team's mixed development project for the Victoria Ward Properties along the Honolulu waterfront. We were in a heated debate regarding the sacrifice of a design feature in order to address a water infiltration issue. Elmer concluded all discussion on the matter with his statement, "To hell with the design feature, you won't be so proud of it after the attorneys have sued your !$## off."

Elmer had quite a reputation at the school. With his silvery white hair, beard, and pronounced eyebrows, he was hard to miss. But most of all, it was his persona that left an indelible impression on everyone he met. First-year architecture students were invited with their parents for orientation session every fall. After the formalities, Elmer would address the incoming students and would let them know they were in for hell and half of them would not survive. Then he would address the parents and inform them that *he* now owned their children's hide.

Elmer had focused his career on technical issues in architecture and had a national reputation as an expert on building diagnostics. He had authored a number of technical books and publications, including *Wood as a Building Material: A Guide for Designers and Builders,* 2nd ed. (Wilcox, Botsai, & Kubler; John Wiley & Sons, 1991) and *Wood: Detailing for Performance* (Dost & Botsai; GRDA Publications, 1990). Needless to say, Elmer's influence on architectural education at the University of Hawaii had a distinct practical bent to it.

Because the real world is full of limitations and the pragmatic reality of difficult clients, liability issues, and technical problems, I frequently hear architects advise architecture students to enjoy their school experience, to experiment with design and creativity. As such, a lot of my fellow students probably shirked off Elmer's comments as pessimistic exaggerations. Personally, I thought of them as challenges. But then my background was somewhat unusual.

Prior to becoming an architect, I taught math and chemistry in high school for three years. With a BS double major in math and chemistry, it was obvious that I had a more analytical nature. Furthermore, I had worked full time throughout my architectural education, project managing and doing construction documentation on a variety of projects. I had to face the realities of architectural practice on a daily basis and was always challenged to produce the best design in spite of them.

After graduating from architecture school, I lost touch with Elmer for seven years. During this time, he retired as dean of the School of Architecture and became "of counsel" to Group 70 International, one of the largest architectural practices in Honolulu. I joined Group 70 in 2000 and worked with Elmer on water infiltration issues on a variety of projects. In 2007, Elmer approached me about the potential of writing a book on water infiltration based on his doctoral manuscript. While there are books that address water infiltration for residential design quite well, he had reasoned that were no current books on this topic focused on commercial design.

Since our firm operates as a group practice, it seemed natural that Elmer and I could not undertake this venture alone. So we recruited two other key members of our team. We structured our team to provide different viewpoints on water infiltration issues so that the book would address a broader perspective. Phil Cuccia represented the viewpoint from the specification writer, Hiram Pajo approached the issue as a construction document production manager, and I took the perspective as a principal architect and designer. Elmer? He provided his sage advice and expertise throughout the process.

To be clear, Group 70 International, Inc. does not endorse this book and has had no part in the formation of its precepts and opinions. The book is private work of individuals who happen to have worked for the same company and wanted to share their thoughts on this important subject with the building industry. The book is not a manual or guideline of operations for, and does not represent the opinions of, Group 70 International, Inc.

The process to produce this book was systematic and sequential. We focused on one chapter or topic at a time. Each author would write about various aspects of that chapter or produce illustrations that communicated their concepts. We met weekly to review the material. Typically, our meetings were focused on critiquing each other's work and coming to agreement on modifications. I often wondered if it was a good idea to have four authors. As a single author, you wouldn't have to argue with three other viewpoints—unless you had multiple personalities. But in the end, I thoroughly believe this process made for a better book, and we each learned from one another.

It is our hope that this book serves as a useful guide for future generations of architects. Those future designers will be faced with ever increasing complexity of issues: technological advancements in building products, new project delivery methods, and the complexity of organic and "green" design. It is our belief that the principles set forth in this book will have relevance in the new paradigm of building design.

Charles Kaneshiro, AIA, LEED-AP

Authors' Biographies

Elmer Botsai, ArchD, FAIA, is a nationally recognized expert in building diagnostics. Mr. Botsai was also a professor of architecture and past dean of the University of Hawaii's School of Architecture. Mr. Botsai is also past national president of the American Institute of Architects, and honorary fellow of the Royal Australian Institute of Architects, Royal Canadian Institute of Architects, and New Zealand Institute of Architects. Throughout his 40 years of professional practice devoted to building technology problem solving, Mr. Botsai has worked on projects throughout the United States and Pacific Rim.

Charles Kaneshiro, AIA, LEED-AP, is a principal with Group 70 International, where he specializes in the design of educational and institutional facilities. He has a BSEd from the University of Michigan and BArch from the University of Hawaii. One of the first Leadership in Energy and Environmental Design (LEED) accredited professionals in Hawaii, Mr. Kaneshiro has extensive experience in sustainable design and is currently the Green Schools Advocate for the United States Green Building Council (USGBC), Hawaii Chapter.

Phil Cuccia, CSI, CDT, is a specification writer with more than 20 years' architectural experience in preparing specifications and construction documentation for a large variety of building types, ranging from $350 million resort developments to $5 million school facilities. Mr. Cuccia has a BS in architecture from New York Institute of Technology and a Construction Documents Technology (CDT) certification from the Construction Specifications Institute.

Hiram Pajo, AIA, is a registered architect in the state of Hawaii with over 25 years of experience in producing construction documents for a wide range of building types. Mr. Pajo specializes in the technical aspects of building design and has served as quality control manager, project manager, project architect, and job captain over his career. He also taught for five years at the University of Hawaii–Leeward Community College associate's degree program in architectural studies.

Acknowledgments

Elmer Botsai, ArchD, FAIA, would like to acknowledge the support of the University of Hawaii School of Architecture; American Institute of Architects; my wife; my co-authors; and my colleagues Jim Nishimoto, Francis Oda, and William Dost.

Charles Kaneshiro, AIA, LEED-AP, would like to thank the numerous mentors I have had over my career. Duane Hamada, Kent Brawner, Chris Smith, Francis Oda, and, of course, Elmer Botsai have each imparted to me a part of their knowledge and wisdom about our profession. I would also like to thank my wife, Faye, and son, Matthew, who have sacrificed a lot of time for me to spend writing this book.

Phil Cuccia, CSI, CDT, would like to recognize and thank my wife, Jennifer, and stepson, Justin, for the continued support, encouragement, and understanding they gave me throughout the writing of this book. I would also like to recognize several of my siblings, Ed, John, and Paul, all of whom work in the construction trades, for keeping me grounded and focused on the constructability aspect of architecture. Finally, to my mom, who passed away during the writing of this text, and to my dad, who is now recovering after a bout with cancer, I would like to dedicate this book for all the love and wisdom they imparted to me and their encouragement to always strive to do my best.

Hiram Pajo, AIA, is very honored to contribute toward the completion of this book and would like to thank Elmer Botsai for believing in me. I would like to express my thanks and appreciation for the several mentors that I've had throughout my career, giving me the skills I now have: Edwin Hayashi, Alan Yokota, Warren Hananoki, Bill Chang, and Milton Matsunaga. My love and aloha goes out to my wife, Stacy, who always supported me, and, of course, my daughter, Morgan, and son, Isaac, for their unconditional love.

Introduction

This book and its views are based almost solely on the field experiences and findings in our combined practice. This single issue of water infiltration has been for years the largest cause of legal action in the construction industry. Recently, microbial growth has moved into the first or second slot of construction litigation. However, a high percentage of microbial growth is often the result of water infiltration (see Figures 0-1 and 0-2).

Studies of building diagnostics have included extensive field investigation, laboratory testing, and research into many areas within the construction industry. The authors believe and have found that all too often members of the construction industry ignore common professional practice or, worse yet, choose lower-quality solutions to meet the building needs. It is also our opinion that with increasing frequency the reason for quality procedures is becoming ignored.

The current high incidences of liability action taken against design professionals and contractors, both general and subcontractors, basically started in the early 1960s. These liability actions have been growing consistently to where litigation is now epidemic in scale. It is clear that the public expects and demands a higher standard of care from all segments of the construction industry. Unfortunately, this condition is exaggerated by the growth of developers, who all too often are primarily concerned only about the initial costs. This condition has been and is helped along by exaggerated claims from lower-quality products. The design profession is also guilty with their all too frequent desire for innovative design and inadequate concern for building performance.

GREEN NOTE

With the emergence of sustainable design throughout the building industry, we have included this notation box within each chapter discussing a relevant aspect of "green" design. These Green Notes will highlight issues and water infiltration challenges to sustainable design.

Recent developments in court actions demand a much surer approach in assessing the social and technical requirements of a building or building complex, especially within the current urban context. This implies

Figure 0-1 Extensive mold growth populates the entire ceiling of this home.
Courtesy: Mr. Terry Brennan

that the architect must have a better understanding of the physical, legal, technical, economic, and social implications that result from decisions made during the design phases. Methods for obtaining and processing relevant technical data to yield rational answers that prevent building failures should be developed by the representatives of the design professions as a means of information transfer.

In today's legal terms, *building failure* no longer solely implies "structural collapse" as was commonly accepted in the not-too-distant past when a direct threat to public safety was involved. The definition of *building failure* is now perceived to mean any component of a building or, more likely, an assembly of components that fail to fulfill the function intended. There are simple failures of construction materials: Concrete cracks (which is normal), paint blisters, checks in hardwood floors, and prematurely rusted metal or electrical short circuits are but a few examples. The subject of building failure in general is so complex that it is necessary to isolate key areas of the topic in order to approach it realistically. One area of building failure that is considered extremely critical and basic to the primary function of architecture encompasses all aspects of keeping the natural elements from invading the integrity of the building envelope, as a means of protecting life, comfort, property, and building contents. Among these concerns, the water infiltration of buildings ranks at the top of the list. This text, accordingly, focuses on the "water problems" of buildings and attempts to address the problem by indicating (1) why failures occur and (2) how they can be avoided.

Finally, we wish to state that the information and opinions in this book, while based on our belief, sound judgment, professional experience, and other sources of information, are only intended to provide general information regarding the subject of water infiltration. Each individual situation is different and requires the consideration of a number of different factors. Even our own professional opinions and designs may differ from the information and opinions contained in this book, depending on the facts and circumstances of each individual situation. Thus, the consideration and application are left to each professional to determine based on the specific facts and circumstances of each individual situation, including but not limited to, the building type, location, environment, and delivery methodology. We hope that this book will help guide designers in producing quality buildings.

Figure 0-2 Water infiltrates a basement of a structure, causing mold growth. *Courtesy: Mr. Terry Brennan*

1

Requirements of Buildings throughout History

The evolving historical development of architecture indicates that the primary function of a building, or building complex, is to provide shelter and protection for the occupants as well as the storage of goods. The fundamental user need indicates that architecture is perceived as a product that is programmed and designed in answer to a set of considerations ranging from environmental and climatological responses to complex social issues. The first primitive man-made shelters developed by society were a direct response to the need for protection from the elements and predators, initially from preying animals and later from rival societies. It was a basic, instinctive response to the fundamental need to protect life and limb by building a symbolic fortress as a defensible space.

With the advance of civilization, society had the means and psychological urge to collect prized and valuable possessions. The primary function of a building as a shelter was extended to the protection of property, essentially personal property that symbolized status and affluence, in addition to personal well-being. In fact, it was and is the sole function of some structures, such as the "treasure houses" of ancient tribes and the "Fort Knox" of today, to protect property from the elements as well as people.

As societies became more sophisticated, buildings originally designed as shelter from the elements, rival cultures, and predators—often human—also had to be planned for comfort and convenience. The more complex and interdependent societies became, and as pressures of population growth

1

resulted in larger areas of urbanization throughout the world, buildings expanded into areas that are more difficult to design for. In many of these highly developed areas, overexposure to the fiercer elements of nature became a critical factor for survival, particularly when a nomadic lifestyle gave way to cultivation and manufacturing as a way of life.

The point being made is that whether the building is protecting the user occupant such as in a housing complex, personal property as in a warehouse, or contents as in a computer center, its integrity from damaging natural elements must be preserved. It must be remembered from the outset that all elements of nature, though nurturing on occasion, are not always benign. This book addresses building design as a function of providing shelter from the elements, primarily rain and wind. Also, while not included in this book, design should address the protection of life and limb from the major environmental hazards of natural disasters, including fire, flood, hurricanes, tornadoes, tsunamis, and earthquakes. These items must also be taken into account as potential disasters on architectural elements.

PAST SOLUTIONS FOR SHELTER AND CONTROLLING WATER INFILTRATION

In all probability, the first conscious act on the part of primitive man in seeking respite from the elements was to stand under a tree. While this provided shelter of sorts, it did not adequately supply total relief and protection. The next level of shelter was found in natural caves, which provided much greater isolation and insulation. When caves and trees were not available, man's first conscious design intervention in creating a viable physical, built environment probably occurred with the creation of "lean-tos" (see Figure 1-1), which were most primitive but effective structures in deflecting the ravages of uncompromising weather conditions.

In early buildings, the primary concern was to keep liquid water from entering. The focus was on how roofs shed water off the building. There was little concern about vapor and air infiltration or water diffusion through walls above or below grade, and therefore not much was done to control these sources of moisture. In fact, moisture problems occurred from the water falling off the roof, wetting the ground at the foundation, and consequently soaking through and up the wall. Castles of the 13th through 17th centuries provided examples of these types of structures (see Figure 1-2). There were no provisions to keep moisture out or glazing systems for that

Figure 1-1 A primitive lean-to structure offering protection from the elements. *Courtesy: Jo Place*

matter. Still, there was some evidence that architects were beginning to derive methods to control excessive moisture, some of which are still used today, albeit somewhat modified with improved materials. Some of these methods include:

- The use of cavity walls to control water absorbed through the wall from rain and the condensation of water vapors that diffused through the wall
- The use of natural hydraulic cement stucco at the base of buildings

While these methods and materials seemed to, at the time, address the immediate problems, we know from past history that they were not without problems. Improvements in systems for handling site water drainage contributed to the control of water damage to the base and foundations of buildings. Other building elements that were developed include:

- Water tables fabricated from granite and dense limestone used to stop moisture from rising up the wall through capillary action and to divert the water draining down the building's façade away from the base
- Damp-proof courses constructed from slate, fired or glazed bricks, lead sheets, and tarred or bituminized building paper
- Synthetic waterproofing (Figure 1-3)

Figure 1-2 Fenestrations of older castles provided little protection from the weather. *Courtesy: Lesley Browne*

Prior to vapor/air barriers and tight, air-conditioned buildings, buildings were often designed to allow air to be pulled through the building by drafts created by the rise of hot air exiting out through attic vents, cupolas, or roof lanterns. This flow of air allowed the building to "breathe" and therefore established equalization in the differential of moisture levels between the exterior and interior environments. While this system is not very energy efficient, especially in colder climates, it is somewhat effective in controlling moisture in non-air-conditioned buildings by allowing the walls to "dry" out.

TODAY'S BUILDING CONCERNS

Today's sophisticated structures, although a far cry from the simple "lean-to," function on the same fundamental principle of "keeping the natural weather out" and "keeping the amenities of man-made weather in." With recent attention to energy and sustainability, the objective of keeping the man-made weather "in" has assumed critical connotations, with computer management systems designed to control inside man-made weather conditions and operate at peak efficiencies. Although both aspects of keeping "weather out" or "weather in" are extremely important to the total design process, the remainder of this chapter will limit itself to addressing the former. Accordingly, the successive chapters will deal with the specifics of keeping water from infiltrating, or penetrating, buildings from the exterior as the primary objective of this book.

Over time, differentials in temperature and moisture levels have become increasingly larger throughout most parts of the United States, and because of this, controlling air and vapor flow through walls and roofs becomes just as important as controlling "liquid" water from entering the building. As materials and technologies have progressed, building envelopes have become well insulated and tighter with regards to vapor and air infiltration (Figure 1-4). These new technologies offer up a wide variety of materials and products, some of which will be discussed in depth in later chapters. These include air and vapor barriers, fluid-applied and sheet-applied membranes, modified bitumen, and thermoplastic polyolefin (TPO) and ethylene propylene diene monomer (EPDM) roofing, to name a few. Some important concerns for the design professional choosing all of these products is how compatible they are and how they interface with one another to become a complete building envelope from the roof to the walls to the foundation.

Figure 1-3 Synthetic waterproofing applied to a foundation wall. *Courtesy: Carlisle CCW*

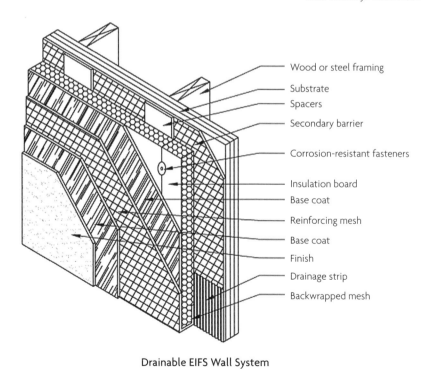

Wood or steel framing
Substrate
Spacers
Secondary barrier
Corrosion-resistant fasteners
Insulation board
Base coat
Reinforcing mesh
Base coat
Finish
Drainage strip
Backwrapped mesh

Drainable EIFS Wall System

Figure 1-4 Current wall system indicating technically advanced layers of weather protection resulting in a "tighter" building envelope *Courtesy: Carlisle H. Pajo*

Figure 1-5 Disney Hall in Los Angeles, California, designed by Frank Gehry, using custom stainless steel wall and roof panels. *Courtesy: C. Kaneshiro*

The complexity of today's structures has been greatly advanced by the development of highly sophisticated digital modeling tools and computerized manufacturing processes. The three-dimensional capabilities of computer-aided drafting (CAD), building information modeling (BIM), and especially Computer-Aided Three-Dimensional Interactive Application (CATIA™) have allowed designers to explore, create, articulate, and fabricate any form in their imagination. Buildings by Frank Gehry (Figure 1-5), Daniel Libeskind, Herzog + de Meuron (Figure 1-6), and others have exhibited what is possible with today's technology. But it also poses numerous challenges for preventing water infiltration. In these complex buildings, it is possible that no two exterior metal wall or roof panels are alike. The question is: How does an architect address the myriad of environmental forces impacting the building? We intend to touch on potential water infiltration approaches to these buildings.

GREEN NOTE

LEED (Leadership in Energy and Environmental Design) is an internationally recognized green building certification system. It is administered by the United States Green Building Council (USGBC) and has become the consensus national standard for the certification of green buildings. The system provides third-party verification of performance standards wherein participants are awarded certified, silver, gold, and platinum certification levels. The USGBC has a membership of more than 15,000 organizations including design firms, manufacturers, developers, and government agencies.

SUSTAINABLE AND GREEN ARCHITECTURE

In the past 10 years, sustainability and green design have become popular buzzwords in the building industry. In the beginning, it was perceived as a fringe element of the design community doing straw bale houses and individuals living off the grid in minimal shelters. But, today, you can barely pick up a newspaper or magazine without seeing a green article or advertisement.

The construction industry has also embraced this trend. The American Institute of Architects (AIA) recognizes the top 10 green buildings annually. There is a plethora of "green" and sustainable design conferences. "GreenBuild," the USGBC's annual conference, is annually attended by approximately 30,000 attendees. It is now rare to find a manufacturer who cannot provide a "green" specification or has not listed the LEED points that their product will assist in achieving.

However, green buildings can create an increase in waterproofing issues. A primary focus of sustainable building design is energy efficiency. A typical strategy to achieve increased energy savings is daylighting. This approach utilizes natural sunlight to replace the illumination provided by artificial lighting. In addition to reducing the power requirements for lighting, this strategy reduces the cooling load for air conditioning and can also result in a reduction of the heating, ventilation, and air conditioning (HVAC) equipment. Benefits of daylighting have been shown to extend beyond energy savings to other benefits such as improved productivity at work and improved test scores in schools.

Daylighting can be achieved through a number of different means whose principal goal is to reflect sunlight into the interior of the building. Reflected sunlight carries only a fraction of the heat load associated with sunlight so the building receives the benefits of the luminance without the temperature increase. One daylighting strategy is to provide roof penetrations over interior building spaces. This can take the form of skylights, roof monitors, and light tubes (cylindrical aluminum tubes with a clear dome; Figures 1-7 through 1-9). The bottom line is that green buildings can have a substantially greater number of opportunities for water infiltration.

Green buildings also encourage reducing the storm water runoff from buildings. One strategy in this area is to provide a "green" roof, which is a landscaped roof that uses plants to consume storm water and thereby reduce runoff (Figure 1-10). This strategy is particularly useful in urban areas

Figure 1-6 deYoung Museum in San Francisco, California, designed by Herzog + de Meuron illustrates the use of custom copper screens. *Courtesy: Sean Gloster*

Figure 1-7 Light collection domes placed on a roof to provide for interior daylighting. *Courtesy: C. Kaneshiro*

Figure 1-8 Exterior sunlight collected from the rooftop domes is distributed through diffuser lenses at interior spaces. *Courtesy: C. Kaneshiro*

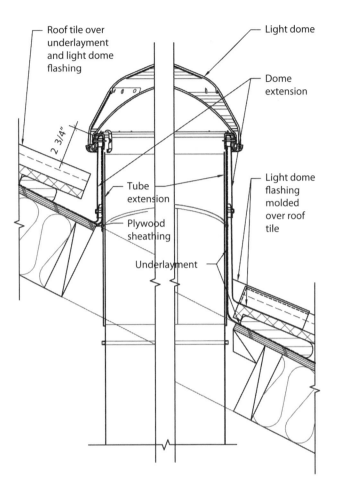

Roof tile over underlayment and light dome flashing

Light dome

Dome extension

2 3/4"

Tube extension

Plywood sheathing

Light dome flashing molded over roof tile

Underlayment

Figure 1-9 Section view at dome and light tube through roof. *Courtesy: H. Pajo*

Figure 1-10 An example of a "green roof" that serves as a roof covering and reduces storm water runoffs from buildings. *Courtesy: Intrinsic Landscaping*

Figure 1-11 Commerzbank Tower Bank in Frankfurt, Germany, by Lord Norman Foster illustrates the integration of the environment with the building environment. *Courtesy: Wikipedia Commons*

where the amount of roof area can exceed open site area. Chicago's green roof grant program, which was started in 2005, offers $5,000 grants to private building owners to green their existing roofs, and has resulted in over one million square feet of landscaped roof space. Obviously, the incorporation of the landscaping on a roof could potentially lead to increased water infiltration issues. Roots from plants can potentially damage waterproofing and exploit hairline cracks into avenues for water. Drainage is an issue as well, with having to design a roof system that will retain water to feed the vegetation and plant covering yet at the same time having adequate drainage to handle the immense amount of water produced by heavy rains.

Whereas the industrial age produced airtight, mechanically ventilated "machines for living," the green movement has given us buildings integrated with the environment. Integration can take many forms and even be the polar opposite of airtight enclosures. Lord Norman Foster's Commerzbank in Frankfurt, Germany (Figure 1-11), relies on natural ventilation and provides landscaped gardens between office floors, hundreds of feet above ground. Needless to say, this type of building provides increased challenges to preventing water infiltration.

Chapter 2 of this book will look at the basic causes of water infiltration in buildings including the effects of wind, thermal and structural movement on design, and moisture resistance.

c h a p t e r

2

Fundamental Aspects of Water Infiltration–Resistant Design

BASIC CAUSE OF WATER INFILTRATION

Water penetrates a building, whether through the roof, windows, walls, or below grade, because of a single physical condition. This condition is a pressure differential between the exterior of the building and the interior of the building. Generally speaking, without differential pressures acting on a building, the potential of water infiltration through walls would be reduced to almost zero.

This pressure differential (Figure 2-1) can be caused by:

- Gravity, such as from debris, ponding water (Figure 2-2), or snow on roofs
- Wind pressure such as on windows and walls
- Water pressure below grade
- Poorly designed mechanical systems

No other force causes infiltration. Infiltration should not be confused with condensation, which is simply cold interior surfaces collecting moisture from internal humid air. Without moisture infiltration either through vapor diffusion or moisture-laden air, there would be no problems with condensation.

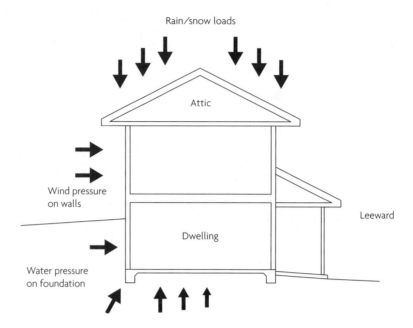

Figure 2-1 Causes of pressure differential on portions of a building structure. *Courtesy: H. Pajo*

Figure 2-2 Extreme ponding of roof due to clogged roof drains or poor slopes. *Courtesy: city of paris @ flickr*

CLIMATE CONSIDERATIONS

In the initial approach to the subject of water infiltration of buildings, one of the fundamental issues that should be addressed is the problem of building exposure relative to the environmental and climatological characteristics of the building site and its surroundings. While one design solution may be adequate for one type of climate or environment, its use in another setting could prove to be disastrous. Before the preliminary designs of a building are even considered, a complete and comprehensive understanding of environmental and climatological conditions of the site is appropriate. It should be developed as an integral part of the building program and thoughtfully considered before any schematic drawings are initiated.

In approaching water infiltration–resistant design, fundamental and primary consideration must be given to storm loads on buildings. It is worth noting here that negative pressures on the lee side or sides of buildings and corners can be up to three times as great as the positive pressures (which causes infiltration) and as such can also have severe structural connotations. Depending on the design of the building, the negative pressure on the lee side can often decrease the building interior pressure, which then increases the pressure differential on the windward side (Figure 2-3). Thus, at extreme levels of pressure, windows on a building are more apt to blow out on the lee side than blow in. That being said, both normal and abnormal conditions must be given attention from the very start in order to gain a thorough understanding of the problem being faced. By reviewing abnormal conditions and correlating them to the worst possible circumstances to be predicted, a more complete and realistic perspective of the anticipated problems will be revealed.

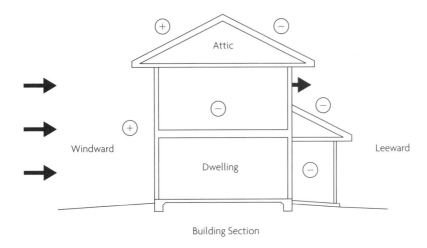

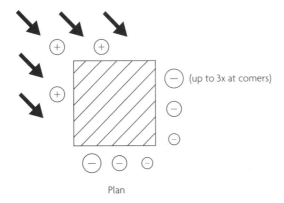

Figure 2-3 Positive and negative wind pressure effect on buildings. *Courtesy: H. Pajo*

In order to achieve this step, the historic record should be consulted not only for data on an annual basis, but also for climatic extremes for the decade and century cycles. Although the 100-year storm cycle may have taken place only last year, and even though the designed life expectancy of a building may be only 50 years, there is no guarantee that the next 100-year storm may not reoccur in another two or five years. The purpose of reviewing the historic record of the 100-year flood is not to determine its time of occurrence, but rather to determine the extreme condition for building performance. The century cycle will establish for the building designer the "outside" parameter, or most extreme design constraints, for which the building will be tested. Design decisions then can be made from this starting point and thoroughly explained to the client from a realistic point of view.

Rapidly changing climatic conditions around the globe is another reason that designers need to verify the environmental data for their project site. Temperature rise, rainfall conditions, and wind patterns are changing globally and cannot be assumed to be the same as a decade ago. To do so could be a grave mistake in building design.

Relevant data on cyclical storm loads can be obtained from the National Weather Service, the National Oceanic and Atmospheric Administration (NOAA) of the Department of Commerce, the U.S. Army Corps of Engineers, and the Federal Emergency Management Agency (FEMA). As these organizations are federal agencies, any reports and technical data published by them is readily available as public information.

In addition to the historic record, it is also extremely important to compare local conditions with regional characteristics due to the fact that there can be significant variations within specific areas. In many regions, there can exist microclimates that vary considerably. Patterns of wind and rain may change drastically from one microclimatic locality to another within the same region. For example, in the San Francisco Bay Area region of California the average annual rainfall for parts of Marin County in the northwest is as high as 44 inches, while for the same region, in contrast, San Mateo County in the southwest, about 15 miles distant, receives approximately 8 inches of rain per year. A more dramatic example exists on the island of Oahu, Hawaii, where the average rainfall in the upper parts of Manoa Valley is as high as 144 inches per year, while four miles away the Waikiki area receives as little as 7 inches of rainfall per year (Figure 2-4). Accordingly, it behooves the design professional to recognize local and regional conditions before starting the design of any structure,

Figure 2-4 Example of
a microclimate in Hawaii.
Courtesy: Michael Allen Turner

whether single-family detached residential or a large-scale commercial building. Consideration of such climatic conditions from the water infiltration point of view can and should influence the building's design orientation, site location, configuration, and architectural detailing. More will be said on this subject in later chapters, but for the moment, the point being made is that comprehensive consideration must be given to existing local variations.

A few words of caution, however, should be given here. It is not sufficient to limit one's consideration only to those existing variations known to prevail in an area; it is also incumbent on the responsible professional to anticipate, as much as practicability allows, any possible future situations that could have a high probability of occurring. The urban fabric is not a static environment, but rather it is constantly subject to growth and change. This is particularly true in this age of accelerated urbanization, dynamic urban growth, and population shifts from one area to another. Current research studies indicate that changes in the built environment do affect and produce climatic and temperature variations within a specific area. There are countless examples in which the addition of a new high-rise building within a city block environment has been known to create new wind, rainfall, and temperature patterns that have affected the performance of existing adjacent structures. If such changes can be anticipated, or their possibility taken into account, a much stronger approach to the water infiltration problem can be taken.

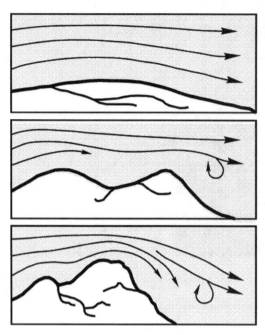

Figure 2-5 Effects of terrain on wind flow.
Courtesy: H. Pajo

SITE CONSIDERATIONS

Relative to site conditions, particular attention has to be given to the configuration of the terrain in which the building is to be constructed. Each characteristic will connote a specific implication on the water infiltration design constraints. Different influences on design must be considered in correlation to terrain distinctions defined by its topology—hills, flat, valley, or plateau—for each will have a different implication as to wind and rain characteristics (see Figure 2-5). An architectural window detail that may be appropriately utilized for a flat, valley area may not be viable in a hilly area due to the change in wind patterns experienced as a normal storm load. Yet some architects have been known to use the same architectural detail in a hill area that was previously successful in a flat, valley area and then wonder why water infiltrated the building. Some of the fiercest winds exist in the Denver plateau of Colorado, and some of the trickiest wind patterns are known to exist in the central business districts of New York and Chicago. Each area has its own characteristics, and each must be studied for its own peculiarities.

There are types of terrain, other than those indicated in the previous paragraph, that have their own distinctive temperament and are more common than realized. One such type is related to the terrain having an ocean exposure as found on the East Coast, the Gulf Coast, the West Coast, Alaska, and Hawaii. An ocean exposure has specific implications for water infiltration–resistant design and normally has a negatively compounding effect on the ability of the building to perform well under storm loads. High winds and saltwater spray form a combination that is most difficult to counteract over a long time period due to corrosion problems incurred by even the most carefully protected surface or architectural finish (Figure 2-6).

Plant materials, existing or new, are also important to water infiltration design in relationship to the fall of the terrain. An existing stand of tall, large trees can provide a windbreak and provide shelter for one building, or it may channel the wind and rain directly into the path of another (see Figure 2-7). Accordingly, it is necessary to study the impact of existing trees on climatic patterns to determine the odds of a future problem, such as new trees installed or the removal of existing trees.

The type of tree should also be a consideration in temperate climates. Because deciduous trees typically lose their leaves during the winter season, this can significantly impact wind patterns. Conifer trees in this climate would be a better choice if the designer wants a more consistent wind block.

In a previous section of the text, a brief mention was made of the importance of studying the impact that an adjacent building or buildings will have on the water

Figure 2-6 Corrosion of Metal Roofing. *Courtesy: H. Pajo*

infiltration–resistant design of the proposed building. Again, this study should not be limited to existing buildings, but must seriously take into account the impact that new buildings might have on the building site. This is particularly true for urban environments for which zoning ordinances allow future high-rise construction even where none exist at the moment. In such areas, particular attention should be paid to street patterns that, in combination with new or existing high-rise development, are known to create a funnel action, with dire consequences for any building in the target area of its path. An architect could be considered acting in an irresponsible manner if his or her preliminary research study ignores this issue.

WIND EXPOSURE

In terms of building exposure, there is a direct correlation between storm loads and their incumbent wind pressure to water infiltration. Wind pressure is without question the single most critical element in water infiltration–resistant design of exterior walls.

The nature of wind speeds associated with storm loads must be thoroughly understood by the building designer so that the implications to building exposures are clear. Weather departments across the nation will quote wind speeds as a matter of course during weather reports announced on a daily basis (Figure 2-8). Wind speeds of 60 to 70 miles per hour are not uncommon during storm loads in many parts of the country. Extreme

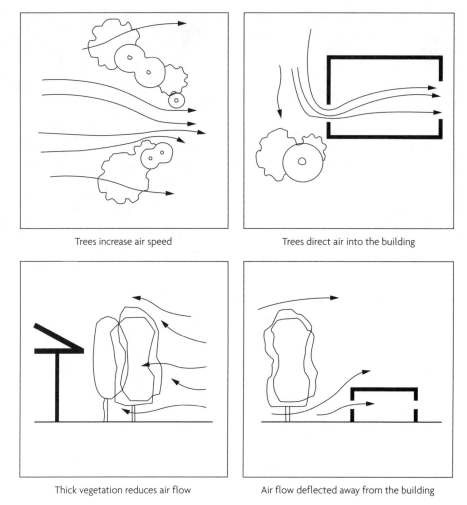

Trees increase air speed

Trees direct air into the building

Thick vegetation reduces air flow

Air flow deflected away from the building

Figure 2-7 Trees affect wind patterns on buildings depending on how they are situated on site. *Courtesy: H. Pajo*

wind loads during critical, severe storms, such as hurricanes, have been known to exceed 150 miles per hour within 30 miles of the center. Published wind data is generally recorded at a 30-foot elevation level. These figures are always low when considering any multistory project. The Uniform Building Code (UBC) and International Building Code (IBC) have tables to cover height variance from wind load. This standard is for code requirements, not necessarily for leak protection.

Gale-force winds are defined as those exceeding 40 miles per hour. Extreme winds are classified as tornadoes or hurricanes.

DATA THROUGH 2007	YRS	JAN	FEB	MAR	APR	MAY	JUN	JUL	AUG	SEP	OCT	NOV	DEC	ANN
APALACHICOLA, FL	54	8.3	8.7	8.9	8.5	7.7	7.1	6.4	6.4	7.8	8.0	8.0	8.0	7.8
DAYTONA BEACH, FL	62	8.8	9.3	9.7	9.4	8.9	8.0	7.3	7.0	8.1	8.9	8.3	8.3	8.5
FORT MYERS, FL	62	8.3	8.9	9.3	8.8	8.0	7.2	6.6	6.7	7.4	8.4	8.1	7.9	8.0
GAINESVILLE, FL	24	6.8	7.3	7.4	7.1	6.7	5.9	5.4	5.1	5.9	6.1	6.1	5.9	6.3
JACKSONVILLE, FL	58	8.1	8.7	9.1	8.5	7.9	7.7	7.0	6.7	7.5	7.7	7.6	7.6	7.8
KEY WEST, FL	54	11.8	11.9	12.0	12.2	10.5	9.6	9.4	9.2	9.5	10.8	12.0	11.7	10.9
MIAMI, FL	58	9.5	10.0	10.4	10.5	9.5	8.3	7.9	7.9	8.2	9.2	9.7	9.1	9.2
ORLANDO, FL	59	9.0	9.6	9.9	9.4	8.8	8.0	7.3	7.2	7.7	8.6	8.6	8.5	8.6
PENSACOLA, FL	43	9.0	9.3	9.7	9.5	8.6	7.6	6.9	6.7	7.6	7.9	8.2	8.8	8.3
TALLAHASSEE, FL	46	6.7	7.1	7.5	6.8	6.2	5.7	5.0	5.0	6.0	6.3	5.9	6.3	6.2
TAMPA, FL	61	8.6	9.1	9.4	9.2	8.6	7.9	7.1	6.9	7.6	8.3	8.2	8.3	8.3
VERO BEACH, FL	24	8.6	9.0	9.8	9.4	9.1	7.7	6.8	6.5	7.4	8.6	8.6	8.0	8.3
WEST PALM BEACH, FL	65	10.1	10.5	11.0	10.9	9.9	8.3	7.7	7.7	8.8	10.0	10.4	10.0	9.6
ATHENS, GA	52	8.3	8.5	8.6	8.3	7.1	6.6	6.3	5.8	6.5	6.6	7.3	7.9	7.3
ATLANTA, GA	69	10.4	10.6	10.9	10.1	8.7	8.1	7.7	7.3	8.1	8.5	9.1	9.8	9.1
AUGUSTA, GA	56	6.9	7.5	7.8	7.4	6.3	6.0	5.8	5.3	5.4	5.6	5.9	6.5	6.4
COLUMBUS, GA	49	7.2	7.7	7.9	7.2	6.6	6.1	5.8	5.5	6.5	6.3	6.4	6.9	6.7
MACON, GA	59	8.0	8.4	8.5	8.2	7.4	6.9	6.6	6.1	6.7	6.5	6.9	7.4	7.3
SAVANNAH, GA	57	8.2	8.6	9.0	8.5	7.5	7.3	6.9	6.7	7.2	7.3	7.2	7.6	7.7
HILO, HI	58	7.4	7.7	7.7	7.5	7.4	7.1	6.9	6.8	6.8	6.7	6.8	7.2	7.2
HONOLULU, HI	58	9.4	10.1	11.2	11.6	11.6	12.6	13.1	12.8	11.2	10.4	10.5	10.3	11.2
KAHULUI, HI	35	10.8	11.3	12.0	13.3	12.9	14.8	15.4	14.7	13.1	12.1	11.5	11.3	12.8
LIHUE, HI	57	11.2	11.7	12.8	13.6	12.8	13.2	13.7	13.1	11.8	12.0	12.4	12.1	12.5
BOISE, ID	68	7.9	8.8	9.9	9.9	9.4	9.0	8.4	8.2	8.2	8.3	8.4	8.1	8.7
POCATELLO, ID	55	10.3	10.4	11.2	11.6	10.5	10.1	9.1	8.9	9.0	9.5	10.0	9.9	10.0

Figure 2-8 A sample of wind speed data by state. *Courtesy: H. Pajo*

Tornadoes are local atmospheric storms of short duration formed by winds rotating at very high speeds, usually in a counterclockwise direction. Tornado formation requires the presence of layers of air with contrasting characteristics of temperature, moisture, density, and wind flow. As a tornado passes over a building, the winds twist and rip at the outside walls, while the reduced pressure in the tornado's eye causes explosive pressure difference between the inside and outside of a building. Tornadoes are extremely difficult to design for and probably need to be limited to unusual buildings.

The hurricane is unique in both structure and strength. On average, the area that contains winds with speeds of at least 74 miles per hour covers some 100 miles in diameter, while gale force winds extend over an area 400 miles in diameter. Such hurricanes are tropical cyclones, formed in the atmosphere over warm ocean areas, in which extreme winds blow in a large spiral around a relatively calm center, the so-called eye of the hurricane. While hurricanes occur along coastal areas, the zone of the highest incidence for tornadoes includes a wide band in the midwest, central, and southern sections of the United States.

As winds increase in velocity, horizontal pressure against structures mounts with the square of the velocity, so that a 10-fold increase in wind speed increases the wind-created force 50-fold. For example, a 25-mile-per-hour wind causes a pressure of about two pounds per square foot, while a wind of 200 miles per hour causes pressure of about 100 pounds per square foot (all with respect to a flat surface). For most structures, such an added force is sufficient to cause a failure of some sort, the least of which is water infiltration. Extreme winds may also produce failure by lowering the atmospheric pressure on the lee side of an enclosed structure sufficiently to cause normal pressure inside the building to explode outward.

At this point it is worth noting that the architect should inform his client about all the design constraints imposed on the building by the climate and the environment. Ensure that the client is involved in the establishment of the level of water infiltration resistance of the various building components. We believe that the amount of money spent on any building component is primarily the owner's choice. It is the architect's responsibility to ensure that the owner has the necessary information required to make prudent decisions in these matters. Such action is not only appropriate; it may keep the architect from future litigation.

In addition to dealing with wind speeds in terms of pressure equivalents, it is necessary to analyze wind effects from three other points of view as follows:

1. Impact pressures
2. Film tolerances of applied finishes
3. Scouring values, particularly in taller buildings

Pressure equivalent implies a steady, even pressure on a surface similar to a constant, uniform load on a structure. An impact load, however, is not constant but rather a dynamic load, which implies a sudden driving force against a component. In engineering terms, a dynamic force such as impact load is known to have up to twice the effect on an element compared to a constant, solely applied uniform load. Thus, from a water infiltration point of view, sudden gusts of wind have a sudden impact force, particularly when it is a rhythmic pulsating force that is known to literally "pump" water past nominal barriers. Accordingly, the possibility of such impact forces acting on a building system or component should be carefully considered.

Finish treatments such as paint and plastic coatings, among others, are intended to protect surfaces by providing a shield, or film, between the surface and outside elements. Once the barrier is breached, water is often free to penetrate these surfaces. The key element in this aspect of water infiltration–resistant design is therefore the effective tolerance of the film itself against breaching forces. Each material used as a protective finish material has its own tolerances and must be examined for its ability to tolerate outside forces as well as the ability to bridge imperfections of the surface it is shielding such as small cracks or nicks. Obviously, if the film tolerance of the protective coating is low, its capability to bridge any gaps will be correspondingly low and would thus be considered a poor water infiltration barrier. Another point that must be considered is the effect of age on the film itself. Many materials deteriorate with age and lose their resiliency and capacities to effectively cover surface imperfections (see Figure 2-9). The critical factors in this case are, therefore, the physical characteristics of the coating used in terms of its tolerance and its ability to perform effectively over a period of time. To hold down initial costs, there is a temptation to use coatings that are less expensive but also less tolerant. Again, in this case, it would be wise to communicate to the client exactly what is being paid for over a long period of time and to apply life-cycle cost analysis as a means of explaining the actual long-term cost/benefits that can be realized by using quality—but more initially costly—materials to do the job.

Figure 2-9 Deterioration of the exterior walls of this older building may cause water infiltration. The exterior skin of the building contributes to protecting the structure. *Courtesy: H. Pajo*

Up to this point in the text, wind has been discussed as if it were a clean and unpolluted element, which, as it turns out, is not the case at all. As proof of this, all the reader has to do is remember the irritating dust blown into his or her eyes during a stiff, heavy breeze. In actuality, wind or even gentle breezes carry many different types of particles in their streams of flow. It is this characteristic of wind that again becomes a critical factor in water infiltration–resistant design.

As the wind carries these particles in its path and they become airborne, it is clear that they, too, will strike any surface that stands in the way. Many of these airborne particles, which are abrasive in nature, such as sand and soils, can be hurled against exposed surfaces with a significant impact force. The combination of the impact force and the abrasive quality of the particles produce a scouring action on the surfaces being struck just as if the surface were being scoured by sandpaper or a household cleanser used to scrub pots and pans. Such action on an exposed surface over a period of time can easily destroy film tolerances and protective barriers applied as a finish coating and strip it clean, thus effectively baring the substrate to potential water infiltration. Building designers therefore must take into account the scouring, abrasive characteristics inherent in wind action. Any building surface or component that is known to be exposed to constant wind action must be treated differently than a shielded surface in order to preserve its integrity in water infiltration–resistant design. There is great variation in the values between the contrasting materials indicated. The architect should be thoroughly familiar with the surrounding environment of the building site and the potential types and sources of airborne particles that can be generated by wind forces acting on building surfaces and components. A quick analysis of such environmental characteristics can be made simultaneously with study of the directions of the prevailing winds and storm winds, which any reliable architect conducts as a matter of course before starting preliminary building designs. Such an analysis could serve as protection to the designer from unforeseen difficulties at a later date, along with providing the client a more durable structure.

In closing this section on storm loads, we will review some of the known facts that have been observed in actual case studies. It is also important to understand that wind forces at higher levels above the ground are generally considerably greater than at ground level. Without a wind tunnel test, it is next to impossible to evaluate the characteristics of wind patterns 300 feet in the air by making a calculated judgment from ground level observations. Because patterns, speeds, and flows at higher elevations may have different characteristics than those anticipated, it is a high priority to conduct wind tunnel tests for all tall buildings. Finally, wind-driven rain, as well as airborne particles, can exceed many paint film tolerances used to protect exposed surfaces. A well-established rule of thumb that all architects should follow is: "If any of the above facts are unknown, or impossible to obtain, the architect should use a large factor of safety." It is worth noting that large factors of safety are not always excessively expensive.

THERMAL LOADS

The thermal load is the main cause of the deterioration and destruction of roofing and wall systems, which are two of the critical barriers to successful water infiltration–resistant design. Thermal loads are the basic cause of complex movements, expansion, and contraction, which are impossible to restrain and most difficult to constrain. Despite any wishes to the contrary on the part of the design professional, thermal loads cannot be eliminated in total, and accordingly must be addressed in one way or another. Table 2-1 gives the coefficient of thermal expansion on several common building products.

A main problem is not one related to the ambient temperature but rather the heat buildup in an exposed material due to solar radiation, which can be tremendous for any given area. In high altitudes and cold climate regions, the ambient temperature can be low, while the heat buildup in solar energy absorbed can be very high. For example, the temperature of exposed metal itself may significantly exceed the ambient temperature. In such a case, the color of the surface itself is critical, for light colors reflect solar radiation and tend to minimize heat buildup, while dark colors absorb heat and are conducive to heat storage and buildup (see Figures 2-10 and 2-11). Solar energy collector panels are designed on this principle to maximize the generation of heating capacities, while for water infiltration–resistant

TABLE 2-1   TYPICAL COEFFICIENTS OF THERMAL EXPANSION

Material	Coefficient	Elongation in 10'0" @ 100°F	Elongation in 10'0" @ 200°F
Aluminum	.0000128	.154" (⅛"+)	.307" (⁵⁄₁₆")
Brick	.0000034	.040" (¹⁄₃₂")	.081" (¹⁄₁₆")
Copper	.0000093	.112" (⅛"−)	.223" (¼"−)
Concrete	.0000060	.072" (¹⁄₁₆"+)	.144" (⅛"+)
Glass	.0000044	.053" (¹⁄₁₆"−)	.069" (⅛")
Plastic	Varies, generally 3–4 times aluminum		
Steel	.0000065	.078" (¹⁄₁₆"+)	.156" (³⁄₁₆"−)
Wood (DF)			
⊥ To Fiber	.000032	.384" (⅜"+)	.768" (¾"+)
‖ To Fiber	.0000021	.025" (¹⁄₃₂"−)	.050" (¹⁄₁₆"−)

NOTE: Surface expansion approximately twice linear. Volume approximately 3 times linear.

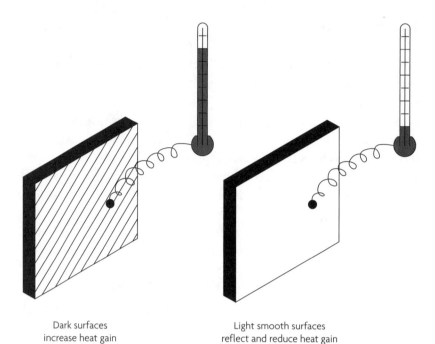

Figure 2-10 Dark and light surface/textures have an effect on the temperature of the material. *Courtesy: H. Pajo*

Dark surfaces
increase heat gain

Light smooth surfaces
reflect and reduce heat gain

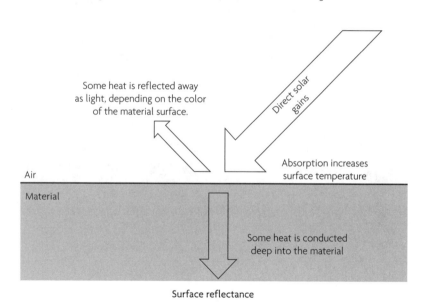

Figure 2-11 Surface reflectance affects the heating surface temperature due to a decrease in absorption at the material's surface. *Courtesy H. Pajo*

Some heat is reflected away
as light, depending on the color
of the material surface.

Direct solar gains

Absorption increases
surface temperature

Air

Material

Some heat is conducted
deep into the material

Surface reflectance

design the opposite is true, as it is best to minimize the thermal absorption wherever possible. In the Sacramento Valley in California, for example, metal roofs exposed to the sun have been known to reach a temperature of 200 degrees. It is not difficult to imagine what the results are in movement for such situations with the potential problems caused by extreme distortion, rupture, or drastic buckling.

Another critical factor in the examination of thermal loads is the range of temperature cycles that take place, not only over a 24-hour period but over seasonal cycles as well. Daily and seasonal cyclical temperature ranges result in constantly changing thermal loads, which subject building materials to significant cycles of movement. On a 24-hour cycle, in some areas, it is possible to have two or more cycles per day. All that is needed is to have a temporary cloud cover or a transient fog layer appear and disappear, first covering the sun and then exposing it once again. Such a phenomenon is not uncommon in coastal zones around the world and certainly can wreak havoc with vulnerable, exposed materials. In places like Hawaii, with bright sunshine interspersed with frequent rain showers, such showers and their rapid cooling effect on exposed building components can result in a multitude of cycles per day. The architect should be aware of such cycles, and particularly in certain environments where two or more cycles per day are frequent. More than a single cycle situation will create much more potential for additional "wear and tear" conditions on all materials of construction.

Thermal loads are responsible for another situation regarding water infiltration–resistant design that relies on the outside "skin" or building envelope to remain functional. It relates to the inside and outside, or internal and external, temperature conditions of a building. For example, consider the situation in a building that has a perimeter air-conditioning system operating full blast for a building in the northern hemisphere in the middle of the afternoon. When the south face of the building is simultaneously exposed to solar radiation, the corresponding heat buildup could result in a 100-degree temperature variation. Additionally, it must be remembered that each building exposure in such situations has a different set of problems that must be addressed. It is well known that such a situation can causes structural change in a building's system, particularly when the structure of the building, as a popular design idiom, is exposed or "expressed" on the outside. In extreme situations, as much as four inches of movement has been recorded on one side of a building with respect to another. The loads, so-called structural loads because they affect the basic structural system of a building, are in reality additional thermal loads imposed on a building. Accordingly, they must be considered not only by the structural engineer but by the architectural designer as well, who is interested in covering all facets of the building process that will affect water infiltration–resistant design.

The effects of thermal action on materials can be disastrous to the life expectancy of a material or its expected performance that in many cases is taken for granted by the designer, who later realizes the critical consequences only after it is too late. In relating to water infiltration–resistant design, it is of fundamental importance never to take anything for granted because the unexpected can always be expected to occur unless all the variations of the problem have been thought through. Refer to Table 2-1 for some examples of the variations in coefficients of expansion and the critical nature of thermal action on common combinations of materials. As can be seen, some materials are extremely vulnerable to thermal action through expansion and may deteriorate rapidly under adverse conditions. Strangely enough, some materials such as single-ply roofing are resistant to moisture and effectively used as moisture barriers in water infiltration–resistant design that are highly susceptible to thermal action.

Some common ratios

Aluminum to glass	3:1
Aluminum to concrete	2:1
Aluminum to wood (‖ to fiber)	6:1
Aluminum to plastic	1:4
Wood (‖ to fiber) to plastic	1:24

As shown in Table 2-1, there can be a dramatic variation in the behavior of building materials with respect to thermal expansion. One extreme exists in comparing aluminum and plastic, in which the expansion characteristics of the latter are three to four times that of the former. When the two materials are used in conjunction with each other, as is often the case in current building designs, it is not difficult to visualize the extreme movement that takes place between the two materials. If synchronized action or guaranteed bonding is necessary between two materials to achieve water infiltration–resistant design, it is obvious that aluminum and plastic are not the combination of materials to use when subject to thermal action.

Thermal action also produces another effect on materials of construction that are left exposed to the direct rays of the sun. In extreme cases, this type of thermal action removes the resiliency characteristics of certain materials and renders them brittle and subject to cracking or disintegration (Figure 2-12). Many kinds of asphalt products or sealant components are susceptible to variations in solar radiation and should be handled accordingly. Materials of construction that require a bonding action between layers, such as certain types of thermal glass, are also sensitive to extreme thermal variations including solar radiation.

STRUCTURAL MOVEMENT

Not recognizing structural movements of a building is also one of the leading causes of failure in water infiltration–resistant design. As indicated in the previous section, thermal action on the structure of a building can be critical to the integrity of water barriers or moisture barriers. Cases have been cited in which as much as 4 inches of differential thermal growth movement was

Figure 2-12 Deterioration is evident on a cracking roof membrane. *Courtesy: Cracked by Heat (pullpulox!!!@flickr)*

recorded between one side of a building and another. Rather than engage in the reading of a repetition of data previously presented, suffice to realize that in this section also, references to thermal loads on buildings imply structural movement that can be critical to water infiltration issues. Such structural movements of a building are in reality produced by differential thermal loads imposed on the building system.

Other than thermal loads on a building, there is an additional range of movements to which a structure is subjected, such as those caused by natural environmental forces. One of these is the effects of wind sway in tall buildings. In some cases, depending on location, it can exceed building sway due to seismic activity acting on the structure. In both cases, due to excessive sway in the upper floors of a multistory building, movements of up to 10 inches in both directions, or a total displacement of 20 inches, have been recorded. In certain instances where the wind has buffeted tall buildings, the occupants have been excused from work and allowed to leave the premises when affected by a motion sickness similar to "sea sickness" due to excessive and continuous building movement. If wind sway can affect the occupants of a building in this manner, one can easily visualize the effects such swaying has on structural systems and components, let alone the smaller architectural members that require a tight fit to preserve the building envelope from water infiltration. In such cases, the critical elements must be designed for relative movement between parts or face the problem of literally being torn apart.

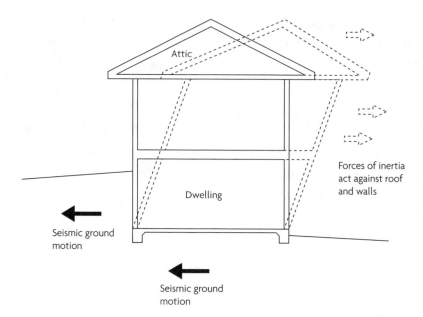

Attic

Forces of inertia
act against roof
and walls

Dwelling

Seismic ground
motion

Seismic ground
motion

Figure 2-13 Seismic
forces at work on a dwelling
structure. *Courtesy: H. Pajo*

Seismic action has a critical difference in terms of building performance when compared to wind action, namely that the action tends to be multidirectional rather than essentially coming from the same direction. Another difference is that rather than exclusively striking the outside of the building as does wind, seismic action affects the entire building, inside and out, simultaneously (see Figure 2-13). Again, in this case, we are concerned with relative movement between components in water infiltration–resistant design, and here, with the current fashion leading to ductile frame design, buildings have been designed to move up to 3 inches in both vertical deflections at cantilever ends. When structural systems are being designed to accommodate elastic/plastic deflections, it is only logical that water infiltration–resistant components be designed on the same basis or otherwise face building failure.

There is another potential building characteristic that the architect must be prepared to confront when dealing with attempts to anticipate problems associated with building movement. It is a direct result of differential settlement at the base of buildings (see Figure 2-14). Settlements that produce a one-inch variation are not that uncommon.

In summary, if the problem could be approached solely from any one of the aspects of building movement described here, it could be solved relatively simply. However, the architect must address the problem from

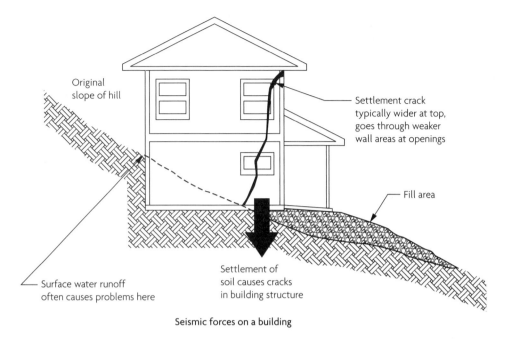

Seismic forces on a building

Figure 2-14 Differential settlement may cause cracks to occur at various portions of a structure. *Courtesy: H. Pajo*

a multidirectional point of view and design component parts in anticipation of any combination of the movements indicated. Combinations of building differential settlement, due to soil liquefication during ground motion, and seismic excitation are already a matter of historic record. Extreme thermal loads accompanied by severe winds that set up an induced swaying motion are also common and require architect accountability. In short, the structural movement of the basic frame of a building can be caused by a numerous set of conditions, and the design professional should be aware of all of them and their various combinational effects in order to establish a viable approach to the problem.

BUILDING CONFIGURATION

The basic configuration of a building, in terms of both plan form and three-dimensional vertical mass shape, also has a direct bearing on certain specific aspects of water infiltration–resistant design. The architect must be aware of the concerns governing building configuration in order to address the problem knowingly. If not considered, surprises can occur after the building is completed and occupied.

The effects of wind loads on a structure will differ considerably depending on the shape of the building (Figure 2-15). However, in dealing with wind loads, the first principle to remember is that the negative pressures acting on the leeward side of the building are usually greater than the positive direct pressure on the side struck by the wind, or windward side. Under such circumstances it is only natural that building failures occur by windows falling out rather than being blown in. Parapets are extremely exposed to these lee conditions. In fact, one of the authors has seen built-up roofing lifted off the roof deck due to the negative vertical pressure adjacent to the parapets.

Perhaps it would help if the architect considered tall buildings as simply an airfoil set on edge. Remember, an airplane flies because of a major reduction of air pressure on the top side of the wing. When considering orientation, a good rule of thumb is "Don't let your building attempt to fly."

In round buildings, a 3-to-1 ratio has been recorded for the difference in wind pressures between the leeward and windward sides of the building. This ratio will vary from building to building, depending on the actual shape. It is important to note that at the corners of the building isolated

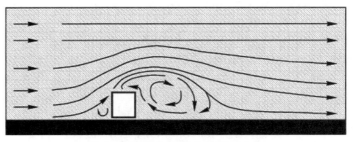

Flow pattern: Side view wind against face

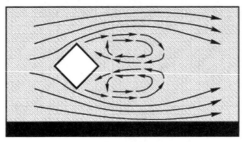

Figure 2-15 The shape and orientation of a building will influence the flow patterns of wind. *Courtesy: H. Pajo*

Flow pattern: Top view
wind against edge

GREEN NOTE

Site design and building orientation are also key aspects of sustainable design. When placing your building on a site, the designer must address a variety of issues including:

- Respecting the natural site features such as habitats, water features, and landscaping
- Reducing the development footprint
- Maximizing open space
- Natural topography
- Maximizing daylighting

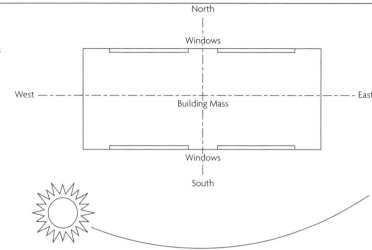

Idealized building massing and orientation to maximize daylighting in northern hemispheres. *Courtesy: H. Pajo*

Daylighting is a key approach to energy efficiency in most sustainable projects. This strategy utilizes reflected natural sunlight to replace artificial lighting. In the northern hemisphere, the predominant concept to maximizing daylighting is to create a narrow building massing orientated on an east-west axis with windows on the north and south face.

---

stresses occur that are different in character, and more concentrated, than those located elsewhere. In addition to such isolated stresses that occur at the corners, a building is affected by other unbalanced loads. The magnitude of these unbalanced loads changes both horizontally and vertically. Changes can occur over a single bay or span, and their differences are even noticeable from floor to floor. The problem is compounded by adjacent buildings or objects that deflect the wind flow and redirect it in another direction to strike an adjacent building in a more concentrated fashion than that of an unimpeded wind load. As a result, the pressure change can be as much as 5 to 10 pounds differential in a single floor or single bay. Thus, the analysis of wind loads on the surfaces of a given building must extend beyond the building itself to determine the effects of adjacent structures or objects on wind flow patterns in order to obtain an understanding of unbalanced wind loads acting on any surface.

When the building is to be located in a seismic risk area, serious consideration must be given to the effects that the building configuration will have on the innate structural stability of the building. In terms of seismic excitation, buildings with symmetric plans are known to perform more predictably because the loads tend to be distributed equally across the building rather than unequally. Such unequal forces tend to cause problems in the design of certain walls and their ability to resist infiltration.

By now it should be clear that differential structural movements, differential pressures, and differential thermal loads are critical factors in the design for water infiltration resistance. The magnitude of the loads is not as critical as these differential movements for the long-term performance of the building components. Differential movements of various components, when not designed for, are known to literally destroy the integrity of an unrestricted system.

Asymmetrical relationships in building structural and nonstructural systems set up eccentric responses that are directly related to the stiffness factor of a structural element or non-structural component. Again, as in the case of wind loads acting on a building, ductile frame building types are particularly vulnerable due to the fact that the system is designed on the principle that the accompanying movement will assist in the absorption of the earthquake loads. While this movement may be appropriate for a structural system, it makes the approach to water infiltration–resistant design somewhat more difficult. Some structural engineers base the structural analysis of buildings under seismic excitation on the yield stress, instead of elastic stresses, capacity of the load-bearing member, which the code allows. This can cause undue stress on the nonstructural, such as the building envelope. It is difficult for the architect to design for the integrity of nonstructural systems performing under such demanding conditions, but it can be done if addressed.

It should be noted that cantilevers are also particularly susceptible to earthquake forces and are known to incur greater movement, due to their free end, than any other structural or rigid element. In design of water infiltration–resistant barriers or elements that occur in or around cantilevered elements, the architect must recognize the magnitude of potential movements and deflections and seek solutions to the problem accordingly. Remember, a series of cantilevers under seismic load can have tremendous compression factor at one floor level with equally tremendous separation factor at the same time.

It is extremely important for the architect to be aware of the possible variations in vertical stiffness ratios that occur in structural design. Again, it is this variation of stiffness ratios that set up differential performance of members and components of a building during stressed conditions.

Architectural components must be designed to take these differential movements into account and cannot be simply designed for a static situation.

MECHANICAL SYSTEMS

Poorly designed or defective mechanical systems can also have an enormous effect on water infiltration. Two major problems are:

1. The lack of makeup or return air for heating, ventilation, and air conditioning (HVAC) and exhaust systems

2. Oversizing of the HVAC system

In fan coil units, negative air pressure caused by the lack of makeup air and the return air cycle, typically through a dropped ceiling plenum, pulls air through the exterior wall of the building and into the wall cavities of the areas being conditioned, which are generally tied into the ceiling plenums. In humid climates this air is typically laden with moisture. When the moisture carried by the airflow reaches the dew point within the wall cavity or ceiling, the moisture will condense to liquid and create the potential for microbial growth. The negative pressure in this scenario can also lead to pulling liquid water and moisture vapor, via diffusion or capillary action, through breaches in the building envelope such as cracks or improperly installed or defective sealant joints (Figure 2-16).

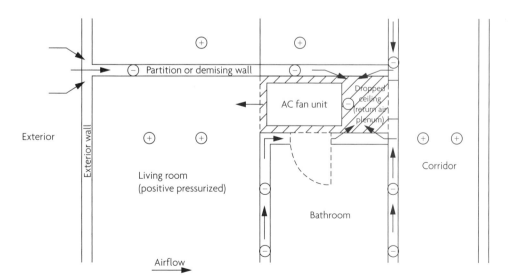

Figure 2-16 Pressure differential illustration as it relates to an air-conditioning unit. *Courtesy: H. Pajo*

Oversizing of HVAC systems is another culprit, giving the preceding example. Oversized units tend to have short duty cycles and therefore cannot properly extract the moisture from the air brought in through the negative pressure as they are designed to do. Bathroom and leaky central air exhausts have similar effects with regard to creating negative pressure in buildings.

GREEN NOTE

Employing natural ventilation in buildings reduces energy consumption and also can improve the indoor environmental quality in buildings. However, designers need to be aware that such approaches can also lead to mold, which is detrimental to indoor air quality and ultimately liability issues. Condensation occurs when moisture-laden air meets cold surfaces. Careful design and coordination with mechanical systems must be executed where these situations occur.

Condensation upon mechanical diffuser and subsequent mold growth around adjacent wall surface. *Courtesy: C. Kaneshiro*

The next chapter addresses criteria used in the evaluation of the different sources of pressure on buildings and how designers should treat these criteria as they relate to the water infiltration strategies.

Performance Criteria and Priorities

PERFORMANCE AND PRIORITIES

The preceding chapters discussed various aspects of a building's exposure and vulnerability to the basic and predominant causes of water infiltration. Once the fundamentals of the problem are understood, it then becomes a matter of establishing priorities and performance standards or criteria. Some trade-offs can be made between the final objectives in establishing criteria and priorities, but it must be made clear that any trade-offs will probably be based on economics and seldom on performance of the solution selected.

It is also extremely important that any trade-offs made for economical reasons must be clearly and thoroughly explained in writing to the client so that all ramifications of the choice are completely understood. In such cases the client should be made part of the final solution. In terms of legal wisdom, this can be accomplished by communicating the design constraints imposed on the development of the building by climate and environment in addition to the rationale behind the final solution selected to solve the problem, including any inherent weaknesses and perceived complications so that the client will know exactly what is being paid for.

This point relative to client participation in specific phases of the design process cannot be overstressed. A thorough and comprehensive explanation of potential hazards of water infiltration problems imposed by a particular site would clearly assist clients or a board of directors to understand what "they are buying" from a cost-benefit point of view and avoid misunderstandings at a later date. All design professionals should take this critical data into account most seriously during the early, initial phases of design. By taking such precautionary procedures with client participation during the early stages of preliminary design, many legal headaches on both sides can be defused before they occur. A straightforward explanation of the options that can be taken as solutions to the problem, with the client making the final decision after knowing what is being paid for, will circumvent potentially explosive problems in later years and avoid legal encumbrances. In our opinion, it would be extremely prudent to record in writing the entire process and results selected.

PERFORMANCE CRITERIA

In Chapter 2 it was indicated that water infiltration is due to pressure differential. Exterior forces, which contribute to this pressure differential, generally come from three sources:

1. Storm loads

2. Thermal loads

3. Structural frame movement

In this chapter, we will look at the performance criteria for each of these sources.

Storm Loads (Wind Loading)

In the case of storm loads, it is first necessary to convert wind velocity to static pressure in order to grasp the basis under which most loads are applied to determine the water penetration of windows, curtain walls, wall systems, doors, and roofs. First, the wind velocity of storm loads common to the area under investigation should be determined. For example, in some environments it is not uncommon to have storm load wind velocities at grades of 60 to 70 miles per hour.

It is important to remember that wind pressures increase in direct proportion to building height. This data should be documented and made part of the performance criteria for the architectural cladding and components expected to resist water infiltration. In converting wind velocities into pressures, there are several methods set forth by the Structural Engineering

Institute in the document entitled ASCE 7-05 "Minimum Design Loads for Buildings and Other Structures." The methods are:

- *Method 1—Simplified Procedure:* Used for structures with a height of less than or equal to 60 feet with a regular shape
- *Method 2—Analytical Procedure:* Used for structures of any height with a regular shape
- *Method 3—Wind Tunnel Procedure:* Used for any type of structure regardless of height and shape

The first two methods determine the pressure through mathematical equations, which incorporate several factors. A few of these factors include but are not limited to:

- *Exposure:* Based on land profile or ground roughness and topography (see Table 3-1).
- *Importance Factor:* Determined by the nature of occupancy of the structure and the type of wind regions in which the building is to be constructed.
- *Basic Wind Speeds:* Wind design speeds assigned to particular regions throughout the country. These wind speeds are determined by collecting the three-second maximum peak gust speeds in miles per hour measured at 33 feet above the ground in the region where the building is to be constructed.
- *Building Height:* Whether the structure is considered low-rise (mean roof height is less than or equal to 60 feet) or high-rise (structures greater than 60 feet in height).
- The openness of the structure, whether it is classified as enclosed, partially enclosed, or open. The definitions and criteria for these terms are given in the ASCE 7-05 and the 2003 or 2006 IBC.

GREEN NOTE

Commissioning is the process of testing, adjusting, verifying, and training to assist the design and construction team to deliver a facility that operates as a fully functional system as per the design intent. Typically, this process is facilitated by a third-party engineer who was not part of the design team. The commissioning agent provides quality control measures, which typically monitor the design, construction, start-up, and operation of the building's systems, mostly mechanical and electrical. The process is initiated by establishing a plan from the outset of the project that identifies performance standards and goals. Enhanced commissioning also includes a review of the design drawings. During construction, the commissioning agent requires witnessing of important components being installed, checked, and started up. Finally, at close-out the commissioning agent coordinates the training of facility personnel to ensure that they are instructed on how to operate the equipment properly. Commissioning has been shown to improve the operational efficiency and life span of building systems. Sustainable design emphasizes the use of performance commissioning for buildings so much so that it has become a growth industry within our current economic recession. Increasingly, states across the United States are considering mandating commissioning for government buildings.

TABLE 3-1 EXPOSURE CATEGORIES

B:	Exposure B shall apply where the ground surface roughness condition, as defined by Surface Roughness B, prevails in the upwind direction for a distance of at least 2,500 feet or 20 times the height of the building, whichever is greater.
	Exception: For buildings whose mean roof height is less than or equal to 30 feet, the upwind distance may be reduced to 1,500 feet.
C:	Exposure C shall apply for all cases where exposures B or D do not apply.
D:	Exposure D shall apply where the ground surface roughness condition, as defined by Surface Roughness D, prevails in the upwind direction for a distance of at least 5,000 feet or 20 times the height of the building, whichever is greater. Exposure D shall extend into downwind areas of Surface Roughness B or C for a distance of 600 feet or 20 times the height of the building, whichever is greater.
	For site located in the transition zone between exposure categories, the category resulting in the largest wind forces shall be used. Exception: An intermediate exposure between the preceding categories is permitted in a transition zone provided that it is determined by a rational analysis method defined in the recognized literature.

Surface Roughness Categories

B:	Urban and suburban areas, wooded areas, or other terrain with numerous closely spaced obstructions having the size of single-family dwellings or larger.
C:	Open terrain with scattered obstructions having heights generally less than 30 feet. This category includes flat, open country; grasslands; and all water surfaces in hurricane-prone regions.
D:	Flat, unobstructed areas and water surfaces outside hurricane-prone regions. This category includes smooth mud flats, salt flats, and unbroken ice.

Information in these tables was obtained from ASCE 7-05 "Minimum Design Loads for Buildings and Other Structures."

The wind tunnel method is a testing procedure that is done in a laboratory with a scaled model of the structure being designed being placed on a turntable in a wind tunnel (Figures 3-1 and 3-2). The scaled model usually consists of the surrounding buildings and terrain. The model is exposed to winds from multiple directions within the tunnel and the pressures are measured by pressure taps that are installed over the entire surface of the scaled model. These measurements are input into a computer from which pressure contour maps and point pressure maps are developed for each face of the building including the roof. The information obtained from this test can then be used by the architect or engineer to design the structural frame and cladding and components of the building.

As it can be assessed from above, calculating the wind loads and converting the wind speed to pressures can be a complicated process especially

Figure 3-1 An elaborate scale model of a city block used for wind tunnel testing. *Courtesy: CPP, Inc. (All materials are covered by applicable copyright laws: © CPP, Inc. 2009)*

Figure 3-2 Wind tunnel testing using high-velocity fans. *Courtesy: West Wind Laboratory, Inc.*

if one is using method 2. For easy of discussion as well as for practical purposes, a general rule to follow is that:

$$1 \text{ inch/head of water} = 5 \text{ lbs. of pressure (lbs./sq. foot)}$$
$$= 45 \text{ mph of wind velocity}$$

Or, to look at it in another way, again in general terms, a wind velocity of:

- 20 miles per hour will push a column of water approximately 1/5 inch vertically.

- 45 miles per hour will push a column of water approximately 1 inch vertically.

- 80 miles per hour will push a column of water approximately 3 inches vertically.

Table 3-2 is a chart indicating a simplified way of converting wind velocity to static pressure in pounds per square feet and in inches of water. The data in this table gives one a quick conversion that is accurate enough to do preliminary calculations. It is strongly advised that the architect consult with their structural or wind engineer in determining the actual pressures for high-rise or irregular-shape buildings.

This table can be used to convert wind velocity (in miles per hour) to static pressure (in inches of water or pounds per square foot).

Referring to static pressure, the implication of this data in terms of water infiltration resistant design is that the window, curtain wall system, or door assembly, utilized in building construction must be so designed and manufactured to resist a column of water pushed 1.20 inches vertically during a 50-mile-per-hour storm wind, or 4.80 inches vertically during a 100-mile-per-hour storm load, and so forth.

What becomes most disturbing to the building designer is to realize that most standard window assemblies including those rated as high performance that are manufactured as stock items for construction do not meet realistic performance standards under critical storm loads in resisting the accompanying static pressures in inches of water being driven vertically. The performance criteria of certain curtain wall assemblies and window and door systems appear highly questionable when tested against real pressures developed during storm loads (Figures 3-3 and 3-4). For example, the American Society for Testing and Materials (ASTM) standard static pressure water testing method for windows, of a 15-minute

TABLE 3-2 WIND VELOCITY TO STATIC PRESSURE CONVERSION TABLE

WIND VELOCITY (MPH)	STATIC PRESSURE (Inches of Water)	STATIC PRESSURE (lbs. per sq. ft.)
5	0.010	.062
10	0.040	.249
15	0.100	.561
20	0.190	.998
25	0.300	1.560
30	0.430	2.246
35	0.580	3.057
40	0.760	3.993
45	0.970	5.054
50	1.200	6.240
55	1.450	7.550
60	1.720	8.985
65	2.020	10.545
70	2.350	12.230
75	2.700	14.040
80	3.070	15.074
85	3.460	18.033
90	3.880	20.217
95	4.330	22.526
100	4.800	24.960
105	5.290	27.510
110	5.800	30.201
115	6.340	33.009
120	6.910	35.942
125	7.500	39.000
130	8.110	42.162
135	8.740	45.489
140	9.460	48.921
145	10.090	52.478
150	10.800	56.160
155	11.530	59.960
160	12.280	63.897
165	13.060	67.953

(continued)

TABLE 3-2 (CONTINUED)

WIND VELOCITY (MPH)	STATIC PRESSURE (Inches of Water)	STATIC PRESSURE (lbs. per sq. ft.)
170	13.870	72.134
175	14.700	76.440
180	15.550	80.870
185	16.420	85.425
190	17.320	90.105
195	18.260	94.910
200	19.200	99.840

Figure 3-3 Window assembly testing at a certified facility. *Courtesy: P. Cuccia*

duration, specified a minimum pressure of 2.86 pounds per square foot, which equals a 0.55-inch static head of water, which in turn approximates a 34-mile-per-hour wind. This has been established as an acceptable standard, yet it is acknowledged that while this pressure may be adequate for products to be used in sheltered low-rise buildings, the accepted criteria are too low for exposed applications where wind velocities are known to commonly reach 50 miles per hour during common storm loads. No wonder standard window assemblies and curtain wall systems in high-rise buildings often do not resist water infiltration at the upper floors!

Figure 3-4 Window failure during a mock-up testing will yield valuable information in preparing for actual building installations. *Courtesy: P. Cuccia*

A designer should realize that each building is unique and that there are situations requiring height performance criteria.

While ASTM standards are the bare minimum requirements, the American Aluminum Manufacturers Association (AAMA) breaks out windows and doors into performance classes: Residential, Light Commercial, Commercial, Heavy Commercial, and Architectural. Each class has a minimum test pressure associated with it. For example, if you take the ASTM minimum static pressure of 2.86 psf, that value falls into the Residential classification, whereas for a window in the Heavy Commercial class, the minimum static pressure is 6.00 psf. The following (in Table 3-3) are the minimum design pressures for each class:

TABLE 3-3 MINIMUM DESIGN PRESSURES

AAMA Classification	Design Load in Pounds per Square Foot	Water Infiltration— 15% of the Design Load (20% for AW classification)	Structural—150% of the Design Load
Residential (R)	15	2.25 psf	22.5 psf
Light Commercial (LC)	25	3.75 psf	37.5 psf
Commercial (C)	30	4.5 psf	45 psf
Heavy Commercial (HC)	40	6 psf	60 psf
Architectural Window (AW)	40	8 psf	60 psf

Water test pressures are based on 15% of the design pressure for R, LC, C, and HC and 20% for AW class windows and doors. In response to the recent hurricanes in the past decade, building codes have become stricter as to the required resistance to high wind loading of the façade components. This has motivated window and door manufacturers to design and develop higher-performance windows and doors to meet these requirements. For example, it is not uncommon to find windows rated under an AAMA classification of AW-80, which is tested for no water infiltration at a static pressure of 16 psf.

The architect should specify and control performance standards and design criteria and not contractors, code bodies, or manufacturers. For major buildings, the design professions should insist on wind tunnel tests for complex site or building configurations as well as exterior façade mock-up testing and field testing. If not, then the only protection left to the building designer is to use a *large* factor of safety or have the owner make the criteria for design. It is important to make sure that any tests used cover all the criteria for high-performance standards.

If reasonable wind tunnel tests are used, they should encompass the surrounding area of other existing buildings, open areas, streets, and the like, and even, where possible, any future changes of the urban fabric, rather than just the designed building alone. All of these factors will influence and/or change the degree of exposure in many critical ways, as discussed in Chapter 2.

Wind loading also affects other components of buildings such as roofing and edge flashings, so much so that building codes have now adopted standards for edge flashing systems used to terminate low-slope roofing systems, in particular the ANSI/SPRI ES-1 2003 standard that addresses coping flashings at parapet walls and horizontal roof edges. This standard considers several factors for designing low-slope roof edges.

- The structural integrity of the substrates to which the coping or flashings are anchored to at the roof's edge
- The wind resistance or uplift resistance of the edge detail
- Material specifications, for example, metal thickness, fastener spacings, and the like

THERMAL LOADS

In working toward establishing criteria to satisfy thermal loads, the architect and engineer must be thoroughly familiar with the building's environmental setting. This is particularly true for foreign work, such as in the Middle East; Southeast Asia, where much work is being developed; and in other areas in which building components can be exposed to a 150-degree variation in ambient temperatures alone.

Movement caused by thermal expansion and contraction or thermal loading needs to be considered in designing building envelope components, including metal flashing, roofing, windows, curtain wall sealant joints, and so on. Because many components that make up the building envelope are fabricated from different materials, it is important to study how thermal loading affects the materials individually and as a whole. For instance, a vinyl window nailed through a nailing fin into a wood stud needs to be designed to compensate for the movement caused by thermal expansion and contraction; usually, this is handled by having elongated or slotted holes in the nailing fin. Another instance would be applying waterproofing to a wood deck and then covering the waterproofing with a concrete topping. If not designed properly (i.e., without a slip sheet between the waterproofing and the topping), the different rates of expansion and contraction between the wood substrate and the concrete topping will ultimately tear the waterproofing to shreds.

Metal gutters, flashing, and roofing splices must be designed with certain dimensional overlaps or expansion joints to withstand the thermal movement within the metal so as to not open the seam or cause buckling and oil canning. Depending on the types of metals used, these dimensions can vary somewhat. The Sheet Metal and Air Conditioning Contractors National Association (SMACNA) set forth guidelines for these conditions in their Architectural Sheet Metal Manual.

Sealant joints are another area of big concern when dealing with thermal movement. When designing for the size of the joint, one will normally take into account the structural movement of that joint, but one also needs to account for the thermal movement as well. In many cases, the structural movement may be greater than the thermal movement, and therefore designing for the greater movement will be sufficient. However, there are situations where both thermal and structural movement is creating a compound load on the joint. For example, where the joint may be expanded from its normal width due to extreme cold temperatures and at the same time forces acting on the building cause structural movement, that joint may very well fail if it was not designed to handle the compound loading or if the sealant specified cannot accommodate the percentage of movement. Temperatures at the time of application also need to be considered. Generally, sealant manufacturers have specific temperature ranges for the application of their products. The design professional should become familiar with this information when specifying the type of sealant to be used in the joint.

STRUCTURAL MOVEMENT

For other types of exposures, the architect must work closely with the structural engineer in clearly identifying the potential structural movements inherent in the structural design and under what conditions. Regardless of what is popularly imagined, most buildings have generally predictable movements. It is best to document and assess them with the structural engineer in order to develop performance design criteria for all elements of the building as a total system rather than a collection of isolated parts. It is important to include the potential of all natural hazards—earthquakes, storm surges, extreme winds, and so on—regardless of their probability, frequency of occurrence, and location in any given area. Historic records indicate that these may occur when least expected.

It is also important for the architect to work with the mechanical engineers to determine what kind of pressure is being established in the interior of the building. We are familiar with too many buildings that developed problems because the building operated on a negative pressure basis and literally encouraged the water to infiltrate. Buildings designed on a positive pressure basis provide positive pressure within the building, which will be of benefit to the water infiltration design. Positive pressure in the building with a static pressure of 0.2 or 0.4 inches of water will help. However, a mechanical system that is shut down at night becomes a neutral component. It is strongly recommended that the outside air used to create the positive pressure be dehumidified and/or treated before its release into the building.

It is also important to remember that when developing criteria for the problem, an all-encompassing approach should be evolved for all potential exposures and not just one aspect of the problem from an isolated point of view. The architect can invariably count on two or more of the design loads and forces working together to cause trouble. Thus, the possibility of a combination of different forces must be expected and considered in any performance criteria established.

At the risk of repeating ourselves, we urge the architect to strongly consider the following points:

1. Review all exposure conditions, potential loads, and procedures used in establishing potential loads so that the client thoroughly understands all the ramifications of the problem and resulting implications.

2. Relate potential performance criteria to the economic implications of the situation. It must be noted that architectural systems with higher performance cost more. All too often, economic decisions made by the architect to save the client money are not appreciated or discounted by the client when things go wrong.

3. Outline possible potential public liability problems or third-party exposure to the client. It would be appropriate to involve the client's attorney in this area. This may help resolve some of the decisions to be made on "money matters" and certainly will save all parties participating in the building development and construction process from facing unproductive, future headaches.

4. Jointly establish proper criteria and priorities for the intended performance standards of the job. If the owner insists on too low a criteria, the architect may be forced to go along with it, but should protect him- or herself by putting it in writing and perhaps seeing an attorney for legal counsel before taking final action.

There is a driving force behind these four recommendations: The one thing the architect can count on is that a building will leak given half a chance. The architect or engineer should *never* try to save the client money *unilaterally* when dealing with water infiltration–resistant design problems and should never attempt heroic solutions, either. Clearly and professionally present the client with options, and let the client take responsibility for cheap work, but in doing so remember to put everything in writing to the client. In dealing with water infiltration–resistant design, *nothing* must ever be taken for granted because that will be exactly when problems will occur. Client participation is one of the keys to a successful practice free from potential litigation.

c h a p t e r

4

Theory of Water Infiltration

The key to water infiltration–resistant design is a thorough understanding of the pressure differential acting on and/or within buildings. The air pressure difference between the interior and exterior of a building is identified as the agent responsible for leaks. *All* leaks—and we do mean *all* of them—are caused by a pressure differential condition. Condensation is not a leak of liquid water but rather infiltration of moisture-laden air contacting a colder surface, generally an internal surface, often caused by the lack of an airtight envelope and mechanical systems.

SOURCES OF PRESSURE DIFFERENTIAL

There are several sources of this pressure. The principal and obvious ones are:

- Water head
- Gravity
- Wind

Other, less obvious but sometimes important sources stem from:

- Inadequate air-conditioning pressures in buildings and negative pressures caused by such items as kitchen and bath exhaust systems.
- The "stacking effect" common in mid- and high-rise buildings.

It is important to remember that these pressures are often combined to double the trouble.

To illustrate the implied meaning of such pressure differential in order to emphasize its importance, even in common everyday usage, the "soda and straw" example can be used to demonstrate basic characteristics. When someone sucks on a straw in a soda pop bottle, what is actually happening is that the pressure in the mouth cavity is being lowered so that it is less than the surrounding atmospheric pressure. It is the atmospheric pressure that causes the soda to go up the straw. To state it another way, it is the difference in pressure between the outside atmosphere and the inside of the mouth cavity that is literally *pushing* the soda up into the mouth cavity to even the pull of gravity. In space, as has been proven during the moon shots, a person could suck on a straw all day and nothing would happen, and is why everything is in squeeze tubes as a means of getting the contents out of containers.

In buildings and other physical facilities, accordingly, it is not the velocity of water or wind striking the surfaces of a building that causes leaks, but rather it is the pressure differential in itself. Water in itself, even though fluid and somewhat viscous, is stable and static and must have a vehicle to carry it through an aperture such as a hole, slit, crack, gap, or other opening. Another simple example is to pour a cup of water out on a level surface and watch. It will spread out until surface tension equals the gravity or head of water. It will then sit there until it evaporates. However, if you lightly blow on the water, it goes all over. Pressure differential. With water, it is the air that becomes the vehicle. If a building contains a flaw in water infiltration–resistant design, the flaw will be found and a leak will occur, provided water has accessibility to the flaw and a vehicle to carry it through the flaw. If water is not accessible to the flaw, then the only thing that will pass through is just plain old air. Accordingly, it is the combination of air as the vehicle and the accessibility of water to a flaw that results in the building failure. At this point it should be stated that while the topic of this text focuses specifically on water infiltration, air infiltration is just as important in building envelope design and needs to be addressed by the design professional. So in order for the building envelope to be complete and efficient, barriers for both water and air need to be in place. In many cases, the barrier membrane used acts as both air and water barriers.

In summarizing the basic reasons for the causes of pressures, which must be anticipated in water infiltration design, the three primary sources are reviewed as follows (see Figure 4-1):

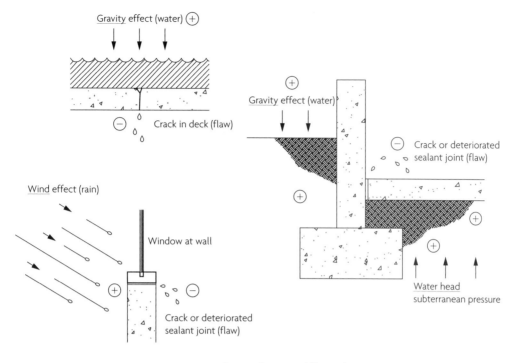

Source of pressure differential

Figure 4-1 Sources of pressure differential on buildings that may cause water infiltration. *Courtesy: H. Pajo*

■ *Water head:* Most critical in creating subterranean pressures, which again is pressure due to gravity

■ *Gravity:* Most critical in creating pressure on horizontal surfaces such as roofs or decks

■ *Wind:* Most critical in creating both positive and negative pressures, or the lowering of pressures, which results in pressure differentials acting on vertical surfaces

HOW DOES PRESSURE DIFFERENTIAL WORK?

For the purposes of this section of the text, a building will be divided into three separate, basic elements critical to water infiltration–resistant design:

1. Horizontal membranes (Figure 4-2)

2. Walls (Figure 4-3)

3. Subterranean walls or floors (Figure 4-4)

GREEN NOTE

Architects should note that some sustainable design strategies create greater opportunities for water infiltration. For example:

- Daylighting and views
- Operable windows
- Green roofs
- Underground parking

It is not to say that these features are not present in nonsustainable projects, but designers and owners need to be aware of these are points of entry for moisture, and design accordingly.

Large windows with operable components provide exterior views and natural daylight to interior spaces. *Courtesy: C. Kaneshiro*

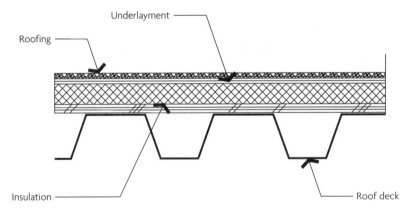

Figure 4-2 Horizontal membrane such as a roof deck. *Courtesy: H. Pajo*

Horizontal membranes consist of roofs, decks, balconies, and other exterior architectural components, which are located above grade. As indicated previously in this chapter, the critical source of pressure differential in such cases is gravity or water head. Wind pressure has little

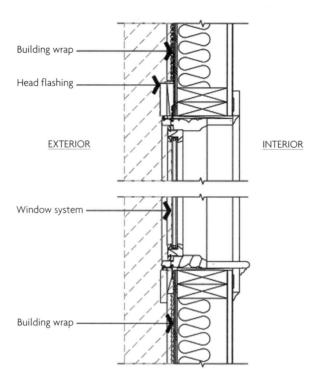

Building wrap

Head flashing

EXTERIOR   INTERIOR

Window system

Building wrap

Figure 4-3 Vertical exterior wall conditions. *Courtesy: H. Pajo*

bearing on the problem in this situation, with the exception of its action through flashing, which will be discussed later.

Here, the quantity of water is a major factor. Negative conditions are aggravated by a pressure buildup directly proportional to the quantity of water standing on the surface. The more water, the more pressure is generated on the horizontal membrane. For example, one inch of water standing on a horizontal surface will generate approximately five pounds of static pressure, while a greater quantity of water standing on the surface will result in a greater pressure. This static pressure in itself is not the cause of leaks, but rather the situation arising from a pressure differential where a lower air pressure inside the building than that outside the building allows the air movement to act as the vehicle carrying the water through any existing flaw and thus produce building failure. Thus, if the air pressure inside the building under the exterior horizontal membrane in the example above is six pounds, or one pound greater than the outside pressure of five pounds standing on the roof or deck above, no leak will occur in terms of water infiltration because all that would happen is that the inside air would escape upward through the horizontal membrane, creating lots of bubbles in the water.

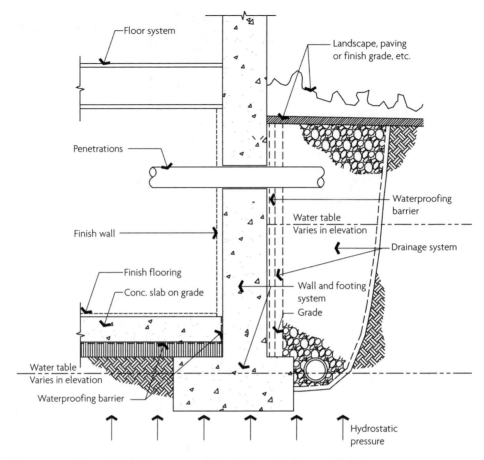

Figure 4-4 Subterranean conditions below grade. *Courtesy: H. Pajo*

However, when the outside pressure is greater than that inside the building, which is the usual condition, the roof or deck *will* leak if a flaw exists in the membrane—the water literally will be sucked into the building. It is simply one of the basic laws of physics in dealing with pressure differentials that all elements will be carried in the direction of least pressure. Accordingly, the water standing on the roof of the building could do nothing else but be pushed in the direction of the space with the lower pressure. Until steps are taken to correct the flaw, or change the pressure differential so that the air pressure inside the building is greater than that outside as generated by the head of water, the standing water by force will continue to infiltrate in the direction of the lesser pressure.

In the case of walls, the principle is the same. During storm loads with a wind blowing against a building and the entire exterior surface sheathed in water, nothing will happen in the way of water infiltration as long as the pressure inside the building, on *all* sides, is greater than that which exists outside. However, as soon as the opposite is true and the pressure on the exterior exceeds the interior pressure, water will infiltrate the building if a flaw exists or the exterior pressure exceeds any water tables on the outside envelope where the critical pressure differential is located.

For exterior wall surfaces, the amount of water cascading down the wall has little effect on water infiltration. A readily observable condition in a leaking building is to observe the water running down the lee side of the building and yet the wall does not leak. The lee side of the build-ing has a lower exterior pressure than the interior of the building. Air is literally being sucked out of the building. Another readily observed condi-tion is the higher level of infiltration in the upper floors of a tall building opposed to the lower floors. The reason is that the wind pressure generally is higher in the upper levels. Therefore, that's the first place to look for leaks. It is only in the case of horizontal membranes and subterranean walls that the quantity of water, which produces the pressure through a hydrostatic effect, becomes critical.

In dealing with water infiltration–resistant design of exterior walls, it is important to realize that the only time the force of gravity becomes a critical influence is after the water has found a flaw in the wall system and made the initial penetration. Then, due to gravity pull, the problem becomes more complex because the origin of the leak is more difficult to find since the water may travel quite a distance before it becomes evident. A classic example of this manifestation, among many others, occurred in an 18-story building in Texas, where severe water infiltration eventually became visible on the first floor of the building by complete saturation of the carpeting for a 12-foot-wide space along the outside wall perimeter. The quantity of water soaking the carpet was so severe that the building occupants actually sloshed through water while walking across the carpet-ing. The leak was finally traced through 18 floors to its point of origin, located along the exterior wall at the ceiling level of the 18th floor just below the roof, or parapet line. The building owners found it incredible to believe that the water had traveled such a distance, but to their relief, once the point of initial penetration was found 18 stories up and repaired, the carpeting on the first floor was no longer saturated and the occupants were able to once again walk across the floor with dry shoes and feet.

To recapitulate, quantity of water is not the major issue for water infiltration of exterior walls above grade. If no pressure differential exists, the exterior wall could be fabricated out of cloth, saturated with large quantities of water, and no leaks would occur, provided, of course, that there are no flaws in the cloth material itself or its splices and joints with other materials. However, such a wall subjected to only to a *light mist* will develop significant leaking when exposed to lots of pressure differential conditions.

Another proof as noted before of this situation is found in the fact that tall buildings are more susceptible to leaks at the upper floors where, although sheathed in less water than the film cascading down the lower floors, the pressure differential is the greatest (Figure 4-5). Accordingly, it is clear that the wind pressure, which causes pressure differentials to occur, is the culprit and not the quantity of water. As the wind pressure increases, the potential of pressure differentials increases, and in turn the infiltration rate increases on a typical wall.

There are two simple tests, which anyone can perform as a practical example of this basic principle. The first is to subject a freestanding 4-inch concrete floor slab to a 3.5-inch water head pressure differential. Leaks will occur in the concrete slab through cracks not even visible to the naked eye. In the second control test experiment, build a box 2' × 2' × 2' in size, as we did, and sheath the outside in gunnysacks. When water is lightly sprayed on the box, it will leak like a sieve. However, under the exact same

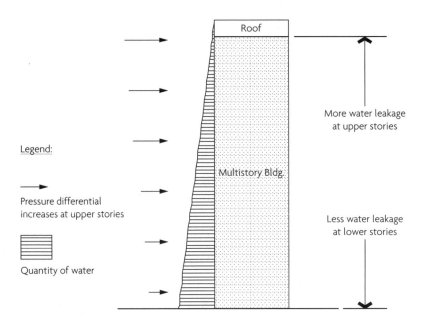

Figure 4-5 Sources of pressure differential on buildings. *Courtesy: H. Pajo*

conditions, if a vacuum cleaner exhaust hose generating one-half inch or more pressure is placed inside the box, no leaks will occur when again lightly sprayed with water. Simply stated, the higher pressure differential inside the box will simply not allow water to penetrate into the interior.

When dealing with subterranean walls or floors below grade, the major cause of infiltration is the pressure on the architectural element generated by quantity of water, water head, and gravity. Below grade on many sites it is not uncommon to find a 10-foot water head, which generates approximately 600 pounds of pressure. Under such conditions, correcting problems due to water infiltration is a horrendous task. There is one aspect of water infiltration–resistant design that must be remembered when working with subterranean components: It is extremely difficult, if not impossible, to correct a mistake made the first time around. It is most important in these circumstances that the initial, original construction be closely supervised and fabricated properly, as this is when water infiltration–resistant design has its greatest chance of success.

It is important to remember that it always costs less to do it properly in the original design. Often, the technical requirements to correct this problem are not difficult. However, it usually costs considerably more to fix a problem than to have it done properly originally.

In essence, gravity will impose a load of approximately 5 pounds per inch of water depth. Therefore, a single foot of water will create 60 pounds of pressure. This force would exceed almost all flashing or other hard conditions except a perfect membrane. In walls, a perfect membrane is never required for water infiltration alone, just enough of a barrier to offset the wind pressure. This is commonly done in low-cost windows that will (hopefully) resist 2.86 pounds of pressure. That's approximately one-half inch of static head, which is achieved by a 35-mile-per-hour storm. This means a 40-mile-per-hour storm will create leaks.

5

Theory of Pressure Differential Plane

Another component of pressure differential design is in the proper location of the pressure differential plane. In water infiltration design, the pressure differential plane is a co-planer barrier in a vertical, horizontal, curvilinear, or diagonal surface that may be utilized to resist water penetration. Within an architectural element, the possibility of having several pressure differential planes exists and each can be objectively identified.

For example, in an unfinished concrete wall without cracks, the main pressure differential plane is the extreme outside surface (Figure 5-1). As we pass through a cross-section of the wall, a series of other differential planes exist until we hit the extreme inside surface, which is a major secondary differential plane of the wall section. Concrete is porous, and as such, it will eventually leak at some pressure. Ultimate porosity will be a factor of density and cost. Hard-surfaced, nonporous materials, such as sheet steel or glass, do not leak under any known conditions.

In porous materials, the major pressure differential plane is right up front at the extreme exterior surface. For our purposes in dealing with water infiltration–resistant design, no others exist.

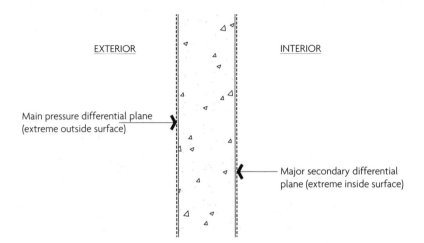

Figure 5-1 Pressure differential plane on a vertical wall section. *Courtesy: H. Pajo*

IMPORTANCE OF LOCATION AND CONFORMITY OF PRESSURE DIFFERENTIAL PLANE

Another key to good pressure differential design is that the building designer must objectively and analytically decide the proper location of the main pressure differential plane to be utilized as the main point of resistance. Once this plane is located it must be carried throughout the entire building envelope. It should *not* be left to happenstance. Once the water breaches the plane, it cannot go back but will continue to move in the weaker direction. Even if the storm stops and no other water is sucked into the flaw, all of the original water will remain in the wall and not filter back out past the initial plane.

A second major consideration that must be given to good design is the unqualified necessity of having absolute continuity in the pressure differential plane (see Figure 5-2). Any breaches must take place in areas where they can be protected, such as at a window or door head condition where adequate flashing and counterflashing will give a fair defense.

It is wise to have the pressure differential plane in a wall as close to the interior of a building as possible. The purpose of this recommendation is that if the water does penetrate the extreme outside surface only to later hit the major pressure differential plane, it will then be possible and easier to get the water out. Becoming more and more common in construction practice today are the components of the building envelope, such as window and door assemblies and wall systems, designed to handle water that penetrates past the exposed, exterior surface. These assemblies

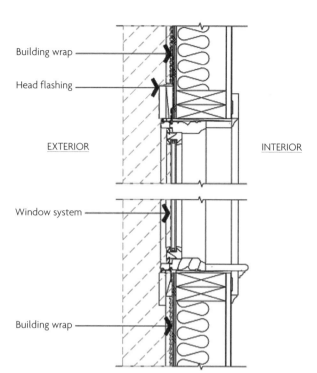

Building wrap

Head flashing

EXTERIOR

INTERIOR

Window system

Building wrap

Figure 5-2 Absolute pressure differential plane of a wall. *Courtesy: H. Pajo*

collect, control, and drain the water back out to the exterior at planned locations. Examples of these systems would be a cavity wall system or a drainable exterior insulation and finish system (EIFS) wall system (Figure 5-3). For window and door assemblies, many manufacturers design the extrusions to include internal gutters and drains or weeps. In the wall system examples, the pressure differential plane is located behind the exposed exterior surface. The thinking is that it is easier to accept the fact that some water will get past the exterior plane and to provide methods of getting that water back out.

Somewhat similar in theory, though diverse in detail, to the one proposed here is for the major pressure differential plane to be placed as close to the interior of the building as possible so that it will be easier to get the water out if there is any penetration. The key is that once water penetrates the major pressure differential barrier at any location, it will no longer go back out past the initial barrier but continue to travel in the weakest direction within the wall, thus making it most difficult, if not impossible, to correct such a condition.

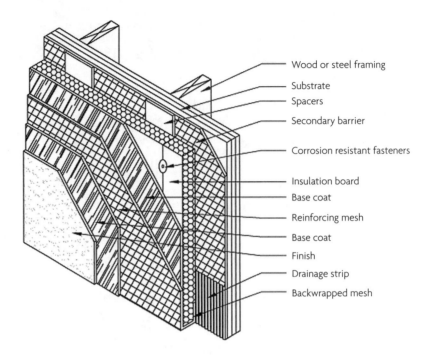

Wood or steel framing
Substrate
Spacers
Secondary barrier
Corrosion resistant fasteners
Insulation board
Base coat
Reinforcing mesh
Base coat
Finish
Drainage strip
Backwrapped mesh

Figure 5-3 Drainable EIFS wall system. *Courtesy: H. Pajo*

RAMIFICATION OF LOCATION RELATIVE TO ROOFING

In dealing with traditional roof systems, there is no realistic choice available in the location of the pressure differential membrane but to place it on the outside surface (Figure 5-4). With some of the new roofing systems being currently developed, recommendations are being made to move the principal membrane into the roof system as an integral component.

As a result of the energy crisis, roofing systems have gone through considerable changes. In order to conserve building energy, it has been discovered that more of the traditional types of built-up roof membranes do not perform adequately as in past years with the addition of insulation to systems where none existed before.

The studies conducted by the National Bureau of Standards (NBS) indicated that this is true because insulated membranes experience far higher temperatures and a far wider range of temperature fluctuations than an uninsulated one. In Europe, fully exposed, dark-colored insulated membranes have been found to be subjected to a range of surface temperatures from −20 to +80°C (−4 to +175°F) and to rapid reversals of temperature of the order to 60°C (110°F). In some severe weather environments such as in Alaska, some tests have indicated that it might be best to

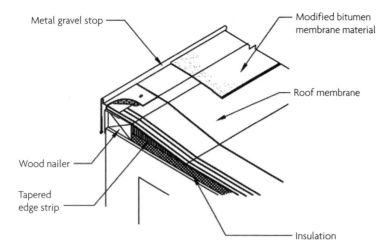

Metal gravel stop

Modified bitumen membrane material

Roof membrane

Wood nailer

Tapered edge strip

Insulation

Figure 5-4 A built-up roof system is traditionally installed on the outside surface. *Courtesy: H. Pajo*

GREEN NOTE

Sustainable design encourages the lowering of building heat and one strategy that is frequently employed is the use of roofing materials with high albedo reflectance. These materials reflect heat rather than absorb it. Typically, this has been accomplished by using roofing materials with light colors or metallic finishes. However, today there are many roofing manufacturers who produce high-albedo reflecting materials in any color, light or dark. Typically, these are for roofing materials that can accept a coating, such as metal roofing. These coatings are also finding their way into the market as wall coatings and, in some cases, pavement coatings.

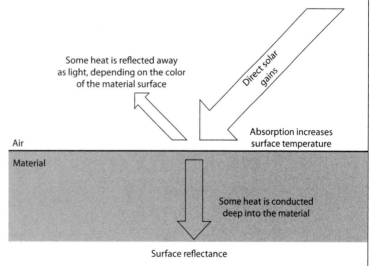

Some heat is reflected away as light, depending on the color of the material surface

Direct solar gains

Absorption increases surface temperature

Air

Material

Some heat is conducted deep into the material

Surface reflectance

Reflectance. *Courtesy: H. Pajo*

place the membrane under the insulation. In this manner the membrane is insulated from severe temperature swings and freeze-thaw cycles.

To state it in another way, the membrane was designed to do only one job—to keep the building dry—instead of the two functions including trying to act as additional insulation on top of the roof deck. It must be pointed out, however, that installation costs for such roofing systems appear to be higher and that precautions taken to protect the membrane from "reflecting" a crack in the deck immediately below it can also cause the membrane to crack and subsequently leak. Accordingly, there is general agreement that the membrane should be in the roofing system rather than being directly and rigidly on the top of the deck surface.

In any event, it is still common practice to rely on the membrane approach, wherever the pressure differential plane is located, to protect buildings from water infiltration through its roofing system. It is extremely important to have no breaks in the membrane for obvious reasons. In fact, there is a tendency among some designers currently to specify huge, single-piece prefabricated membranes in order to reduce the number of splices, which are potential weak spots in a membrane system and reduce field costs. According to the General Services Administration (GSA), the roof is one of the most trouble-prone components in a building.

RAMIFICATION OF LOCATION RELATIVE TO EXTERIOR WALLS

Turning to subterranean walls, it is not economically feasible because of complicated installation details to place the pressure differential plane on the inside, except in corrective work, where there are few choices. In normal above-grade construction, the membrane should always be placed immediately under the outside weather surface (Figure 5-5). For example, in light wood frame or metal stud construction, the membrane is placed under the outside weather surface but over the studs, whether it be plaster, shingles, wood or aluminum siding, or plywood. To move it inside the outside face of the studs would expose the studs and lead to complications. When placed directly under the outside weather surface, the shingle or plaster gets rid of about 90 to 95 percent of the water and the membrane is reduced to only taking care of the small, remaining amount. Such an example is the mark of a good decision being made on the location of the pressure differential plane, which acts as the principal membrane.

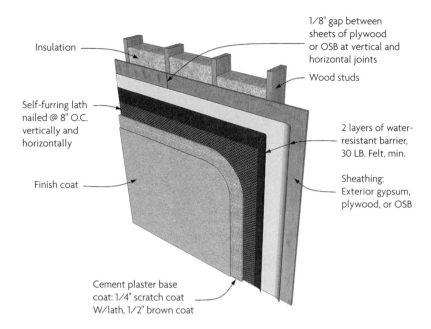

Insulation

1/8" gap between sheets of plywood or OSB at vertical and horizontal joints

Wood studs

Self-furring lath nailed @ 8" O.C. vertically and horizontally

2 layers of water-resistant barrier, 30 LB. Felt, min.

Finish coat

Sheathing: Exterior gypsum, plywood, or OSB

Cement plaster base coat: 1/4" scratch coat W/lath, 1/2" brown coat

Figure 5-5 The membrane applied to the exterior side of the wall system will provide an efficient barrier to water. *Courtesy: International Masonry Institute (IMI)*

When working with masonry wall systems such as cavity wall brick construction, which was used extensively in the past, traditional methods functioned very well when the pressure differential plane was located on the inside of the wall. In the old days, brick masonry walls were furred and plastered inside with a hard-surface cement plaster or Keene's cement finish. Such a skim coat of plaster did not act as a membrane but rather as a pressure differential plane because its application ensured an airtight barrier; with no vehicle to carry the water inside, the walls remained dry. Now it is popular to expose the old brick by sandblasting the walls, which all leak because the pressure differential plane formed by the skim coat of finely applied plaster has been eliminated. A good coat of paint on the inside would tend to serve the same purpose as the plaster skim coat, but because it is currently *de rigueur* for building designers to have exposed brick as an inside wall surface, such buildings often leak.

For metal wall systems, the pressure differential plane can be located anywhere. In corrective work, it is easy to drill holes into the outside face of the metal systems to get the water out. This method has been extraordinarily successful in correcting water infiltration by equalizing the pressure inside and out so that the water can escape to the outside, which is similar in principal to the European approach described earlier.

The major problem with all wall systems, whether they be aluminum or plywood, is at the intersection of different materials, intersections of different systems, and intersections of similar materials. It must be emphatically stated that in dealing with water infiltration–resistant design, the architect must be aware of the critical nature of the fallibility of intersections, intersections, intersections!

6

Applications of Horizontal Asphalt Membranes

hapters 4 and 5 presented the basic theory in water infiltration and pressure differential planes. Some of the fundamental issues of water infiltration–resistant design were analyzed in order to give a substantive understanding of the essential aspects of the problems facing the architect. It is the intent of this chapter and the next to present information on the application of actual systems that, hopefully, will help keep the architects from facing problems later. The respective data to be provided is addressed on a "how to do it" basis.

ROOFS AND DECKS

Basically, both roofs and decks have identical problems in dealing with water infiltration–resistant design except that decks are normally more difficult to handle due to their increased exposure to traffic and abuse. However, in general, the basics underlying each application are similar; accordingly, in this chapter, both will be discussed on the basis of standard-type operations and the design constraints involved.

Hot-Mopped Systems

The first operation presented is the typical "hot-mopped" system so prevalent on many buildings throughout the country.

Currently, there are several bitumens available from which the architect may choose. All, or at least most, of them offer a good membrane system for the money. Most prominent of these systems are the:

- Traditional asphalt hot-mopped system
- Newer, modified bitumen hot-mopped system (SBS)
- Torch-applied system (APP)

We are now seeing a new generation of coal tar systems, many of which claim to equal the old coal tar. For finishes, gravel is still widely used in built-up roofing applications, whereas mineral cap sheets are used more often in modified bitumen systems. We will not attempt to cover each of the systems, as that would take a stack of paper at least 1 inch high. Instead, some general comments will be offered regarding issues that generally are appropriate for all hot systems. It is also strongly recommended that the architect be aware of and use the latest edition of the National Roofing Contractors Association (NRCA) Roofing and Waterproofing Manual. In this manual, one will find more information and knowledge than anyone can use.

The shape, size, and condition of the substrate are critical factors in determining what horizontal membrane to use. Generally speaking, large, open (uncluttered), simple shapes of low slopes are most appropriate for hot-mopped, built-up membrane. Hot systems on steep slopes are difficult to properly install, and roofs with excessive penetrations don't work well for this system. While these installations can be done, they are fussy and difficult. Odd and complex shapes again are not appropriate, as they require excessive care with edge conditions. One will be better off looking at other systems in any of these conditions.

An initial point that must be made relative to hot-mopped systems is that many professionals, including the authors, are convinced that performance and/or guarantee bonds are an absolute waste of money. It is firmly believed that bonds really don't buy the owner any significant protection and tend to be simply a declining rider to an insurance policy. With inflation, and by the time the client or architect actually experiences a failure in the system, there is such a small return on the original investment that everyone would be better off to call for just a good warranty. Admittedly, the roofing contractor operating on a thin margin does not like to work under such restraints, but any reputable firm will not object to reasonable conditions.

Substrates

Regarding hot-mopped roofing applications, there are some of misconceptions concerning the substrate cleanliness. Adequate broom cleaning, more than anything, is sufficient and satisfactory for most jobs, as long as there are no damaging projections.

One thing that is generally not taken into account when dealing with the application of hot-mopped systems directly to the roof deck is that all systems in this category of roofing installation are applied over substrates that move. One thing that can be counted on is that there will be movement in one way or another in the substrate (Figure 6-1). Wood and metal, for example, will be subjected to movement caused by wind or thermal loads, and concrete will creep over time and crack or move under stresses induced by lateral, seismic, and thermal forces. For this reason, the authors do not like a solid mopped roof under any circumstances.

When movement occurs under a solid mopped membrane, one of two things will happen:

1. A separation of adhesion between the roof and substrate will occur, which, fortunately, solves the problem in itself by now having the roofing system in a position to accommodate future movements.

2. A cohesive failure will take place within the roof system.

Solid mopped roofs applied directly to the structural roof deck are subject to question and are disliked by many professionals who have developed an aversion toward them over years of practical experience because of the

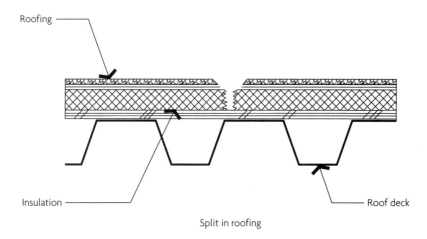

Roofing

Insulation

Split in roofing

Roof deck

Figure 6-1 Movement in the roof substrate may cause splitting or tearing of the roof membrane. *Courtesy: H. Pajo*

potential of cohesive failure inherent in the system. At this critical juncture, it is not uncommon to have considerable movement take place due to the potential for movements and deflections derived from loads applied to the structural components of the building system. Such movements as those encountered under these conditions are known to literally "chew up a roof something fierce," particularly when it is a solid mop situation.

As indicated earlier, a critical concern that deserves careful consideration and supervision is that the substrate must be as free from projections as possible. This includes situations encountered in concrete slab construction, such as stone pockets and "fins." Anything that has the potential of acting on the membrane system as a cutting edge must be avoided and corrected before any sheets are applied. Beyond this concern for projections and cutting edges, and as long as the substrate is broom cleaned, there is little else remaining that requires extreme caution.

The one exception to this, however, is found in substrates of concrete construction, which must present as dry a surface as possible, which concrete seldom is. In tropical and high humidity areas such as Hawaii, Florida, and some zones in the Northeast section of the United States, it is doubtful that the concrete substrate is ever dry, and when dealing with lightweight concrete, one can almost guarantee that it never is. In such situations that involve lightweight concrete, it is next to impossible to have a dry surface, and under some circumstances it is flat out impossible to have anything that even approaches a dry condition.

Because of today's economics, most of the lightweight concrete installations during construction are pumped into the formwork. In order to pump and lubricate efficiently for easy pouring, it is necessary to saturate the aggregate. To do that sufficiently means the moisture content, excluding high levels of plasticizers, is at levels way above and beyond those found in conventionally poured stone concrete. It has also been discovered that lightweight concrete systems, and in particular those laid over a steel deck, will hold moisture for many years. Blisters have been seen appearing on reroofing jobs that replaced damaged membranes on lightweight concrete installations known to be over six years old. In any climate that has an appreciable amount of humidity, lightweight concrete may never dry out. All too often after a new roof has been installed, it can blister and fail due to the moisture still remaining in the concrete substrate (Figure 6-2).

When dealing with such moisture conditions as those known to exist in lightweight concrete substrate, there is only one possible solution to the problem, and that is to design a system to adequately vent out of the

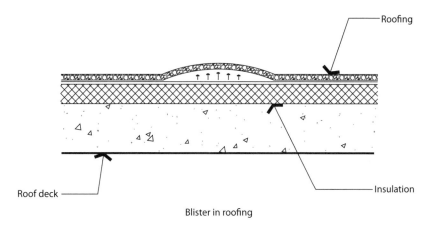

Roofing

Roof deck

Insulation

Blister in roofing

Figure 6-2 Moisture caught in the roof substrate is not desirable where the moisture expands and causes blistering. *Courtesy: H. Pajo*

substrate or be prepared for roof blisters to appear and failure to occur quickly thereafter. Even then, blisters will tend to recur.

It is therefore of great importance to determine whether there is moisture in the concrete. This can be achieved in many ways:

1. A reputable testing laboratory will place a dish of calcium chloride on the deck and cover with a plastic bubble, as described in ASTM F 1869, "Standard Test Method for Measuring Moisture Vapor Emission Rate of Concrete Subfloor Using Anhydrous Calcium Chloride"; obtain a reading on the rate of vapor transmission; and conduct a very sophisticated operation in obtaining the data.

2. Moisture detection devices (Figure 6-3) are also widely used for testing the concrete substrate for moisture and alkalinity. There are several types available; some give more accurate and meaningful results than others. Some of the more accurate types include:

   a. In situ–type probes where test holes are bored into the concrete substrate to about 40 percent the substrate depth, in which a sensor probe is inserted and connected to the lead of the meter to obtain the moisture reading. This testing is done in accordance to ASTM F 2170, "Test Method for Determining Relative Humidity in Concrete Floor Slabs Using In-Situ Probes."

   b. Insulated hood relative humidity meters, where an insulated airtight hood is placed over the bare concrete substrate and a reading is taken from a meter attached to a probe that is inserted into the hood. Typically, the hood is left in place for a period of 48 hours prior to taking any readings. ASTM F 2420, "Standard

Test Method for Determining Relative Humidity on the Surface of Concrete Floor Slabs Using Relative Humidity Probe Measurement and Insulated Hood," is the guideline for performing this test.

3. A simpler approach, which we have used successfully on occasion, is to put down about a square yard of black polyethylene film over the concrete substrate, tape the edges, and allow it to sit through a couple of hot days. If, after that period of time, upon removal of the polyethylene film, any moisture resulting from condensation has collected on the inside surface, there can be no doubt that too much moisture exists in the slab. Although this test admittedly is very simple and a pseudo-scientific device to employ in such a situation, it is a very effective one. The implications of excessive moisture content in concrete substrates, and its potentially critical consequences to water infiltration–resistant design, cannot be overemphasized.

Another major substrate concern is the application of a hot system directly to a wood deck. If there are any joints in the wood deck, never allow hot bitumen to be applied directly to the deck. The hot bitumen will pass through any crack and ruin whatever is below the joint. Always put a barrier such as a mechanically fastened dry sheet or proper board insulation over the wood.

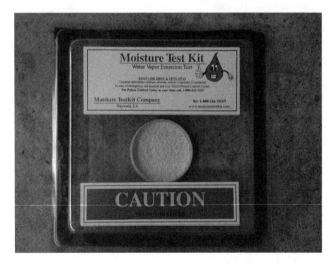

Figure 6-3 Use of a moisture detection test kit is a reliable method of detecting moisture in the roof or flooring substrate. *Courtesy: Moisture TestKit Company*

Insulation

The second major common issue in hot systems is insulation. It is our opinion that organic fiber units should never be used, whether asphalt coated or not. First of all, in many cases, it is extremely doubtful that it can be installed correctly without puncturing the asphaltic coating somewhere. In addition, it would be an unusual system if some edges of the sheets didn't have to be cut, thus exposing raw unprotected edges, in order to fit the actual roof size encountered. There is no effective way to seal these unavoidable field cuts, and as moisture vapor infiltrates and collects in the cuts, up

GREEN NOTE

Green roofs are a growing feature in the sustainable industry. Aided by government incentives like Chicago's green roof program, designers and owners have been implementing these roofs in increasing numbers. However, the introduction of plant material on roofs has its own set of challenges:

■ Increased loading factors

■ Potential for root structures to damage waterproofing or exploit cracks

■ Inaccessibility of roofing membranes

■ Maintenance and upkeep of landscaping

An example of a "green roof" that serves as a roof covering and reduces storm water runoffs from buildings. *Courtesy: Intrinsic Landscaping*

■ Retaining moisture or introduction of water by irrigation

■ Warrantee concerns between landscape and roofing material

However, manufacturers are also recognizing the growth of this market and have been adjusting for it. Hydrotech and Carlisle both have introduced integrated green roof systems. These systems provide a soup-to-nuts approach to green roofs that includes the roof membrane, drainage systems, protection, ballast, soils, and landscaping. The entire system is warranted to avoid liability concerns.

to 70 percent of the insulated value can be lost in a short time. Through experience, the authors have developed some personal qualms over the indiscriminate use of plastic foams now available on the market.

For those practicing in Hawaii or the Gulf Coast states, remember that fiber insulation board is food that termites love. This is another reason why we do not recommend fiber insulation.

Another consideration that must be given to the use of specific foams in roofing situations is the effect that their use will have on fire-rated roof assemblies. Care must be taken in situations under which foam products can be used and under what conditions because many of them adversely affect the owner's insurance policy rates.

It is our opinion that closed-cell insulation is the proper material to use. However, with hot systems, it is essential to use a product that will take hot asphalt. There are two ways this can be done: (1) by using a material that is inherently capable of receiving hot asphalt, or (2) by using a material that has a protective skin, such as aluminum foil, over the closed-cell plastic. In any event, get something in writing that says the particular insulation is satisfactory for hot installations. Again, if used over concrete, use and install insulation that will allow moisture vapor to move laterally without damage to the membrane.

Wherever possible, use more than one layer of insulation and make sure that the insulation joints are staggered in both directions. This simple act improves the insulation overall value considerably.

Finally, it is our opinion that in all conditions, the architect is better off if the insulation board is mechanically fastened to the substrate. It solves many potential problems. Also, remember that at the perimeters of most roofs, particularly those with parapets, the negative uplift forces can be three or more times as strong as the positive horizontal wind forces. An improperly fastened first ply is a potential disaster. In today's current building codes, roof perimeters and edges in high-wind regions are required to comply with ANSI/SPRI ES-1.

FELTS

In the case of felts, we prefer the modified bitumen felts. Most mod bit felts have a glass scrim for strength; be sure the felts are equally strong in both directions. There are some new mod bit series that are not glass, and the architect should look carefully at them. Again, NRCA has some excellent information on them.

Insist that all rolls of felt are round and not elliptical in cross-sections. Make sure all felt rolls are stored on edge. This is necessary to get a quality built-up roof. It is not possible to roll out an elliptical roll and get a uniform thickness of hot asphalt between the felt sheets. This unevenness can and often does cause future problems.

Asphalt

All membrane systems, including built-up roofs, are susceptible to failure because of unequal thicknesses occurring in their cross-sections. Therefore, it is recommended that the felts be rolled directly on the asphalt, rather than the practice sometimes used by contractors in which the felts are rolled out to one side and then slid over the hot asphalt. As found through practical experience in the field, the latter practice is fraught with potential problems. It may work well for small roofing sections but for large, running roofs it represents potentially a bad situation. All too often, wrinkles result that are next to impossible to get out and then end up being permanently "creased" into the roofing system. This often results in serious cracking. Finally, quite often, portions of the asphalt cool down and preclude proper felt embedment.

Glass felts have an important positive attribute: The fiberglass felts will not hold moisture. In extreme conditions, they can be laid and installed between showers if the surface of the deck can be kept reasonably dry. If a roof has to be put down in wet weather because it is imperative to close in a building to meet a stringent construction schedule, it is possible to violate all principles of good roofing practice and lay a glass roof down that will hold for a couple of years. In order to do so, however, it is critical to get the asphalt just a couple of degrees of this side of flammability and so hot it drives out almost all moisture in the glass felts as well as most of the surface moisture of the substrate. A membrane with some integrity will result but it will not be a proper long-life roof.

The lowest-melt hot bitumen possible should be used. It is also very apparent that asphalts from different areas of the globe perform at different levels of quality and workability. Where possible, try to use asphalts that are produced in a good asphalt location.

It is absolutely incumbent that there be a thermostat in the asphalt kettle. It is additionally worthwhile to have a good thermometer in the same kettle because thermostats have a habit of malfunctioning or giving out. In any event, it is extremely important to measure the heat of the asphalt. We strongly suggest that any kettle that does not have a thermostat and a spot for a thermometer should not be allowed to stay on the job. Simply stated, if the asphalt is overheated, its life will be tremendously altered and the properties of the asphalt significantly modified. While it is true that overheated asphalt is much easier to apply on the job, the extreme heat destroys the oil in the asphalt and reduces its attributes as a roofing compound.

If the asphalt is underheated, improperly embedded felts will result, leading to roof ply delaminations. Underheated asphalt does not bond adequately to the layers of felt. In the same way, it is not permissible to have half-full asphalt buckets with semicool asphalt sitting around on the job waiting for the next application of felt. Problems with poor adhesion and poor embedment, again, will follow and lead to eventual failure. The solution is to require that all asphalt in buckets left over from a previous application of any complete layer be poured back directly into the kettle rather than being left around the job site.

PROTOCOL

It is crucial to set the proper standards at the beginning of any roofing installation, and most particularly at the start of any hot-mopped job. Without question, a hot-mopped system is a dirty, grubby job and a trying situation for all concerned. Nobody really likes to do it, so the fewer misunderstandings at the very start, the better for everyone involved. Nothing should be put in the specification that is not intended to be enforced on the job. Accordingly, it is most critical that the right weights are maintained and also critical that job supervision is strongly established on the very first day for all aspects of the roofing installation. This tells the contractor that you want a proper job.

If it is determined that the contractor is not doing the job correctly, it is essential that the job be stopped immediately rather than waiting for the job to be completed, only to indicate later that a mistake was made and that the job will have to be done over. Architects and engineers should not be in the business of playing games. That should be left to others. What we are interested in is getting the job done right with the fewest problems for all concerned.

On any major jobs, the architect should never rely on a manufacturer's representative for inspection responsibilities. It is much better to have a full-time, impartial, and independent inspector. With all due respect to some of the manufacturers' representatives—and there are many good ones—their prime responsibility is to the subcontractor, for that is who buys most of their materials. The amount of materials specified by architects in comparison to those specified by contractors is quite small. Accordingly, the manufacturer's representative is not likely to take the side of the architect against the contractor in anything but the most blatant case. If a full-time inspector can not be afforded, then the architect should be on the job frequently for the first couple of days and later for many short, infrequent, but unspecified intervals for the rest of the time.

If the contract agreement specifies that samples are to be taken during installation of the roof or membrane system, be sure that they are taken. Again, do not play games with the contractor by putting all kinds of requirements in the specifications that the architect does not intend to enforce. The contractor will come to the conclusion very rapidly that such stringent requirements are nothing but hogwash and quickly presume that the entire specification is not that important.

On the finish of a hot-mopped system, there are advantages and disadvantages in using a mineral cap sheets; however, we believe that the pros outweigh the cons. It is known that cap sheets tend to deteriorate faster than top sheets with gravel ballast, they discolor with standing water, and they become soft over time, but the fact remains that it is possible to find a mistake more easily and quickly if there is a cap sheet. Accordingly, this gives a cap sheet installation a basic advantage over other finish systems in that the discovery of future failures is facilitated, and that is one big advantage when dealing with roofing systems protecting interiors with contents of high economic value. It is correspondingly much more difficult, if not impossible, to find a mistake in a gravel surface. We don't recall how many hours have been spent on hands and knees on a gravel surface—in several cases coming off the job with almost bloody knees—trying to find a failure in a built-up roof.

There are clear advantages and disadvantages to using a cap sheet roof. One disadvantage is that cap sheet systems have a shorter life expectancy, but they have a distinct advantage in ease of repair, which can pay off in the long term. Another advantage is that once the cap sheet begins to deteriorate, it is very easy to put another cap sheet over it and get an additional 7 to 10 years' worth of life out of the original roofing system. This cannot be done easily with a gravel system without a "hell of a lot" of expense. It is certainly not realistic to simply put down another flood coat of asphalt and another layer of felt over the original gravel. In addition to the preceding, on high-rise jobs with extreme wind currents, it is possible to save the client from significant trouble by using cap sheet installation rather than exposed gravel systems. Savings are often realized by not having to engage in a reroofing situation after the gravel has blown off the existing roofing system. Cap sheets also avoid payments for the repainting of cars or window replacement, especially in high-wind and hurricane regions where high winds can pick up the gravel and spray it all over the streets below and into the windows of neighboring buildings. This has occurred more frequently than realized in windy areas like Chicago, San Francisco, and Denver and hurricane regions along the Gulf Coast. It is important to use as heavy a cap sheet as possible in order to provide the longest roof life realistically possible.

The authors would never use a glazed system, no matter what any manufacturer claims about the system. It is simply too difficult to do a job

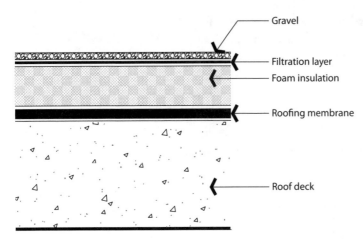

Gravel

Filtration layer

Foam insulation

Roofing membrane

Roof deck

Figure 6-4 Using an "upside-down" roofing versus a traditional type may be desirable in certain applications. *Courtesy: H. Pajo*

that has the correct amount of asphalt to form a finish coat that will not alligator rapidly. Finally, glazed systems simply do not hold up in heavy sun locations.

Many years ago, a system that was used successfully entailed the use of foam glass insulation on top of the roof membrane (Figure 6-4). We are now witnessing a rebirth of that system. Several manufacturers are recommending its use. It is necessary to consider their use in this chapter in relation to their application—it is obvious that such systems have a great potential. Many architects should be looking at these systems for utilization in large-scale roof systems. Although we have not looked at all of them in a critical assessment, there is one concern that architects should be aware of. It relates to the fact that some of the details reviewed indicate that at the perimeters of the system, the membrane is allowed to come out from behind the protection of the insulation. This sets up an unfortunate situation because it allows the membrane to be subjected to a high magnitude of thermal differentiation by going from straight sun exposure to an area under insulation. There is no doubt that the insulation should be carried out to the perimeter, completely over the roof membrane, until it can be tucked under the counterflashing.

FLASHING

In proportion to the entire roofing system, the flashing is very small. However, improperly designed or installed flashing details have resulted in many roof failures, especially at parapet conditions. Flashings will be discussed in more detail in future chapters but we shall touch upon it in this section.

It is disastrous today to attempt to use metal in a hot roofing system when it is integrally built into the roof. This does not include piping or metal vents that go through the roof, or two-foot square sizes of metal, as they are insignificant. What is critical, however, is the continuous, running piece of metal typical to normal flashing situations encountered everyday in roofing procedures. There are very few cases where self-flashing cannot be used in a hot-mopped system, whether it be at an edge or parapet condition.

The differential thermal movement of an 8- to 10-foot length of metal flashing due to thermal load far exceeds the ability of hot-mopped membranes to tolerate. Also, the scissor action at a sheet metal splice will actually cut the felts in two. On most jobs that have been inspected having embedded metal flashing, the felts have been ripped at the point where the sheet metal splice is located. There is little reason to spend money for sheet metal, which is becoming increasingly expensive, or to put a joint in a membrane when it is not needed. Valley flashing of metal simply should not be used in built-up roof conditions. There are many ways in which the roof edges can be finished and self-flashed without the use of embedded metal.

If metals must be used in conjunction with built-up roofs, then without qualification, stay away from highly expansive materials like aluminum and copper. Aluminum is an absolute disaster because in comparison to the thermal expansion, differential between aluminum built-up roofing materials is much too great. Common old galvanized iron sheets are the best choice. Metal can be used as a trim piece or a counterflashing just as long as it is independent from the movement of the roof and not bonded through hot mopping into the roofing membrane as an integral component.

Lest there be some misunderstanding, metal counterflashing is perfectly acceptable and works extremely well. The caution being presented here is that metal should not be layered between the roof plies.

If metal flashing *must* be attached to roofing plies in exceptional situations where the needed detail can be solved in no other way, then the full membrane should be put down first, the metal set on top in a cold asphaltic cement, and finally two or three plies set over the metal to hold it in place. Although some of the last plies may crack or tear, at least the integrity of the membrane underneath will be maintained. Under this situation, the leg of the metal sitting on the deck side should be a minimum of 6 inches long. Additionally, the three plies placed on top of the metal and roof membrane must be feathered (Figure 6-5) so that each ply has at least a couple of inches of clean metal and roofing to adhere to as an extra precaution against slight movements. In this way, the metal is being isolated somewhat from the membrane, although no guarantees can be given that the system will survive under all conditions. Chances are that it

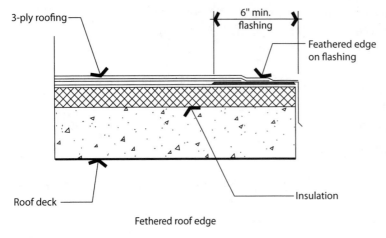

Figure 6-5 Feathered edge roof flashing. *Courtesy: H. Pajo*

will fail, too, but at least the critical membrane will have a very good chance of surviving for its intended life.

Under all conditions, there should be at least a lap of four to six inches on any metal joints with a minimum of three strips of butyl tape between the metal lap to act as a water barrier. Soldered joints must not be used under any conditions without any provisions for expansion to take place without tearing the roofing system apart. All these precautions might seem insignificant to the novice, but it is much better to anticipate where the problems will occur and try to solve them beforehand rather than sit back and wait for the problem to occur. At that point, it not only will be too late, but also will become more difficult to correct.

In the next chapter, we move from the multiple-layer built-up system to single-membrane systems of single-ply and elastomeric.

7

Plastic Membranes

There are basically two types of plastic membranes currently in use: single ply and elastomeric. Both membranes have strong points as well as weak ones.

The first group that has achieved nationwide acceptance in the United States is the single ply. There must be literally dozens of different types currently on today's market. The more common types are:

1. Chlorinated polyethylene (CPE)

2. Chlorosulfated polyethylene (CSPE)

3. Ethylene propylene diene monomer (EPDM)

4. Nitride thermoplastic alloy

5. Polyisobutylene chloride (PIB)

6. Polyvinyl chloride (PVC)

7. Thermoplastic polyolefin (TPO)

Most if not all of these seven basic types are available as reinforced or unreinforced. Their ranges are from as thin as 20 mils to over 100 mils. Their variation in tensile strength also varies widely. Most come in roll goods in a wide range of widths.

They can be installed in a fully adhered manner or spot mechanical fastenings. Their joints can be welded, glued (or sealed), or mechanically connected. Their color range is truly astounding, with a rather good track record for colorfastness.

It goes without saying that large, regular-shaped roofs with few penetrations are the most conducive to minimizing failures and should be the goal on every project. However, the reality of building design will require situations where architects are faced with small, irregularly shaped, low-slope roofs with many penetrations. In such a situation, it is our opinion that an elastomeric or single-ply roof is better suited than built-up systems. The reasons for this are:

1. Elastomeric or single-ply roofing requires *no* cant at curbs; making installation around multiple penetrations and around irregular-shaped perimeters much simpler than built-up (Figures 7-1 and 7-2).

2. Elastomeric or single-ply roofing has a single flexible membrane or roofing surface that can conform to irregular-shaped corners and perimeter jogs much easier than built-up.

Another benefit of single-ply roofing is that it can literally be installed in a rainstorm, which makes it an appropriate choice for a variety of climates

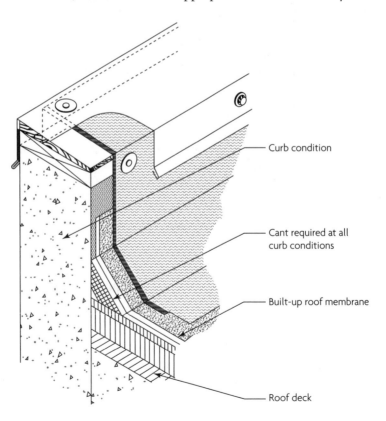

Figure 7-1 A built-up roofing illustration indicating a requirement to use a cant where the roof meets the wall condition. *Courtesy: H. Pajo*

Curb condition

Cant required at all curb conditions

Built-up roof membrane

Roof deck

Built-up Roofing

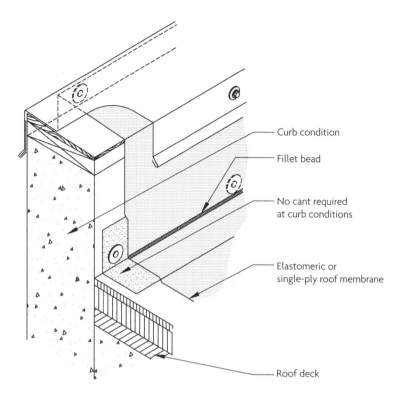

Curb condition

Fillet bead

No cant required
at curb conditions

Elastomeric or
single-ply roof membrane

Roof deck

Figure 7-2 Elastomeric and single-ply roofing is highly desirable where there are many penetrations on a sometimes called "busy" roof. *Courtesy: H. Pajo*

and seasonal situations. With proper venting there is no reason not to use single ply in inclement or highly variable weather conditions.

The material's name, "single ply," clearly articulates one of its major drawbacks. There is no redundancy in a single-ply installation. Frankly, we have never seen a failure of the basic sheet. All products appear to have a high level of material uniformity in thickness, strength, and color. Unfortunately, any error in workmanship automatically results in a failure to stop infiltration. All failures seen by the authors have occurred at parapet conditions, including parapet corner conditions, penetrations through the sheet goods, and a failure of seams (Figures 7-3 and 7-4).

Some manufacturers' representatives have told us that single plies usually have an initial shrinkage factor, in one case up to 4 percent. This is simply unacceptable and incompatible with a quality job. We also have some concerns about single-ply's thermal coefficient of expansion. There simply seems to be no redundancy in these systems to handle the preceding concerns. Some manufacturers are addressing these concerns, and better products should be seen in the near future.

Figure 7-3 Roof condition well suited for elastomeric and single-ply-type roofing. *Courtesy: C. Kaneshiro*

Figure 7-4 A roof condition that has many penetrations through the roofing membrane. *Courtesy: C. Kaneshiro*

The second group, elastomeric materials, is currently one of the fastest-growing segments in the construction industry. The true test of elastomerics is not whether they will stretch but whether they will recover. The overwhelming types of elastomerics are polysulfides, urethanes, and silicones. These are the basic systems to be addressed in this chapter.

The first order of business regarding elastomeric systems is the consideration of moisture. An elastomeric system should not be put down on a wet substrate, period—end of discussion!

Of course, it has been done, but in every case known to us it has blistered and failed. The only way that it can be used is to put a topping slab over it with a slip sheet between the membrane and the topping slab and in conditions where it doesn't matter if total adhesion is lost in the process. For all other general situations, it is imperative to have a dry slab that by description is "bone dry" in order to avoid blistering. If the deck is wet, as described in the preceding condition, and a topping slab is put over the membrane, then an escape mechanism must be designed into the system for getting rid of the moisture vapor that will be generated in the basic slab under a hot sun, or it will develop enough pressure to even lift the wearing slab.

The use of common types of elastomeric system over a lightweight concrete roof under any condition is not recommended. Having said that, it must be recognized that there are some new mixtures of elastomerics

GREEN NOTE

The use of skylights, light monitors, light pipes, wind turbines, and photovoltaic panels in sustainable projects typically increases the amount of roof penetrations. Designers need to be mindful of the selection of roofing material, depending on the quantity and location of these penetrations.

Low-slope roof with mounting brackets for photovoltaic panels and light pipe penetrations. *Courtesy: C. Kaneshiro*

coming on the market. One of the most exciting is the epoxy urethane combination. They have such tremendous adhesion that they have the potential to work on wet concrete that does not have a metal deck supporting the concrete.

SUBSTRATE

In the use of elastomeric systems, the substrate must be absolutely clean in contrast to the condition described for the hot-mopped systems indicated earlier. The manufacturers desire perfect adhesion with the substrate, and therefore want the deck clean. However, if cleaning is required by the manufacturer, there is only one way in which it will be possible: to scrub it with methyl ethyl ketone (MEK) or equivalent. Also, high-pressure water washing appears to be an excellent method, although it must be clearly stated that the deck will require sufficient time to dry out before the application of the membrane. The roof will not be acceptable if it is merely broom clean or anything similar to it. If the roof has to be clean, be sure that it is cleaned properly; otherwise, don't even bother to call for a cleaning in the specifications. Anything short of scrubbing it with a chemical solution or cleaning agent using dry and clean cotton rags will not be acceptable when using elastomeric systems. The rags must be clean and constantly thrown away when dirty.

If the elastomeric system is being put down on a wood deck, the joints must be taped. Although it is possible to shoot a gun-grade sealant into the cracks and joints, most architects have more faith in taped joints. It is possible to have an adhesive failure and still have a raw edge that may have movement in it, but tape will prevent rupture even if it delaminates.

The issue of cleaning is of particular importance when applying an elastomeric system over a balcony condition. Movement from constant foot traffic necessitates the proper adhesion of the material through the deck surface. If the substrate was not adequately cleaned, there is a higher potential of adhesion failure between roof deck and membrane.

One additional step is required and that is the priming of all those critical conditions and openings. The rest of the deck can be thoroughly broom cleaned. The objective method is that when a crack occurs or when a wood joint moves, a loss of adhesion becomes desirable in that the membrane will not be subject to undue tearing or ripping stresses. If a blister or small bubble does occur when adhesion is lost, that particular section can always be cut out and patched while the integrity of the entire elastomeric roofing system is maintained. In the case of exposed deck conditions, the entire deck surface must be properly cleaned using MEK or equal. These areas should also be primed. It is also essential that the deck be smooth. No projections or pockets. Also, all joints or cracks must be properly prepared.

Thicknesses

Fluid-applied elastomeric should be uniform in thickness. It is extremely critical that some system be used during the installation by which a uniform gallonage of coverage is assured and verified. It is preposterous in an elastomeric roof to have close variations, which range from 30 mils to 50 mils or more, and not expect failure (Figure 7-5).

When the manufacturer's sales representatives visit offices, they have been known to bring a fine sample of the membrane in the form of a film 20 to 30 mils thick that, when stretched and held up to the light, is beautiful and clean. What is not indicated is that the sample was cast on a smooth, clean sheet of glass in a controlled laboratory condition where everything was perfect but does not come close to approximating the rough conditions normally found on the job site. In contrast, a fine,

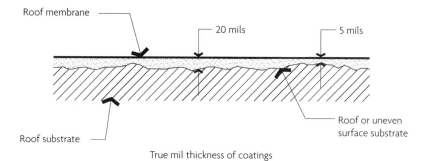

Roof membrane

20 mils

5 mils

Roof or uneven
surface substrate

Roof substrate

True mil thickness of coatings

Figure 7-5 An illustration of
how fluid-applied systems may
vary in mil thickness. *Courtesy:
H. Pajo*

steel-troweled concrete slab has at least 20 mils of surface variation.
A wood float concrete finish will have in excess of 100 mils in surface
variation and be considered acceptable in its own right. A raw wood surface will have variations in excess of 50 mils, and sand-blasted steel is
about 40 mils.

Obviously, it is sheer folly to put down a 20-mil coating on surfaces
that, in contrast, look like the Himalaya Mountains and are 50 mils high.
Accordingly, anyone who puts down a film less than 80 mils thick on any
surface is probably asking for trouble. We try never to use anything less
than 80 mils thick, and in several cases have put down elastomeric coatings
having a thickness of 150 mils. This is in contrast to most manufacturers'
recommended thicknesses of 20 to 40 mils, which we believe is marginal
to properly do the job. It is a very expensive material. Many manufacturers
are interested in stretching it as far as possible to appear competitive in
price with other systems. Obviously, this is misleading, particularly when
variations in the substrate are taken into consideration. The basic problem
is that when the material is fluidly applied over an uneven surface it is not
uncommon to have some areas with 20 mils of coverage adjacent to areas
or spots with only 5-10 mils. This happens as a result of the material's
excellent surface tension, which tends to seek its own level. It is only natural to expect that the 5-mil thickness will be quickly ground off by anyone
walking over it, and a failure may occur in a short time. Some other points
that the design professional needs to be aware of are:

- The manufacturer's recommended thicknesses are typically average
  thicknesses over the entire substrate, meaning that some portions
  of the roof will not have the amount of coverage stated and in fact
  will be less. This is why we recommend applying double the thickness as that recommended to ensure that the areas that receive the
  thin coverage are within the acceptable thickness range.

- Many manufacturers' data sheets indicate the thickness as wet film thickness (WFT), whereas we recommend specifying the thickness in dry film thickness (DFT). We do this because, unless the product being applied is 100 percent solids (usually two-part or multipart systems), it will contain a vehicle component that will flash off as the membrane cures, thus reducing the membrane thickness from what it was when first applied.

- Most products will require that the installation be done in several coats to achieve the required thicknesses. Most fluid-applied roofing membranes are applied at a rate of 1 gallon for every 100 to 150 square feet, which translates to 15 to 25 dry mils. This rate may differ depending on the porosity of the deck.

As with hot-mopped systems, sheet metal flashing should not be used with elastomeric systems for the same reasons indicated previously. Most elastomeric systems are self-flashing systems, so in a proper job there is seldom need for metal flashings.

A good, general rule of thumb to use in dealing with elastomerics is to first determine or anticipate the maximum possible movement, deflection, or expansion, under any condition, and then make the thickness of the membrane three times for large cracks and four times for small cracks. For example, if there is a shrinkage crack in concrete, which under thermal conditions is estimated to move about 15 mils, at least 60 mils of elastomeric material should be used. If a wood deck under wind load or earthquake excitation may move one-sixteenth of an inch, the elastomeric should be at least three-sixteenths of an inch thick.

Market Availability

One of the biggest problems with elastomeric materials is that in many cases the claims for a particular producer is excessive. As it is a relatively new material with many untried characteristics, it is often touted as a wonder material, which will cure all membrane problems. Some manufacturers are making claims that border on defining the process as a miracle system. Representatives, in trying to sell their product, make claims that are simply unfounded.

The only defense is to document all the figures and claims made by the manufacturer's representative and, after a period of time, write a letter to the manufacturer, preferably to someone with some authority such as the president, setting forth how the material will be used on a specific job. Further state that you believe this is in conformance with the information and recommendations given by the representative, who should be mentioned by name and date of visit. The letter should include a request that the manufacturer review the proposed details and advise the office if there is any reason that the given product is not satisfactory for the use intended. It is amazing how many times an answer will be received indicating different requirements for the material's use. In some cases, the manufacturer is never heard from. Obviously, under such circumstances, the "miracle" material should be "deep sixed" and not used.

Of the three materials mentioned, polysulfide has been available longest, and under the right conditions still provides excellent results. It generally needs to be applied fairly thickly. As a matter of fact, it has been most successfully used on jobs such as shower pans. Many polysulfides are able to take prolonged submersion without problems. In a house remodeling on an exposed hill in the San Francisco Bay Area, a wood deck was added to the living room space that incorporated a brick floor that the owner wanted extended to cover the deck. The plywood substrate was coated with about 60 mils of polysulfide to form the membrane and allowed to cure. Then a final coat of 15-mil-thick polysulfide was applied and the brick set into it before it cured. The brick was set with tight butt joints without mortar. The job is now over 30 years old and no problems have been encountered or reported despite the severe location.

Urethanes offer systems that are good but generally expensive. One of the oldest and best is a coal tar urethane, which can be put down in three 50-mil thicknesses and will provide a very good membrane. The disadvantage with the product is that it comes in only one color—black—and is rather soft. As the market expands, the chemistry for urethanes will keep improving. One excellent example is the epoxy modified urethanes. Depending on the design needs, there is undoubtedly a quality material available at a reasonable cost.

The newest elastomeric membranes readily available are the silicones. The good ones are quality material. The only drawback from our standpoint is their expense, which seems to preclude an adequate thickness. The material may perform as claimed but manufacturers' instructions reduce the margin of installation error to zero. We strongly believe thicker multipurposes are more appropriate. As technology improves, this will probably be the material to pay attention to.

In spite of their spotty record, we are very impressed with many elastomerics and have generally had a high degree of excellent results. There are a few requirements that, if followed, yield quality results. They are:

1. Find a quality manufacturer and establish a level of trust both ways. Make sure you understand cohesive, adhesive differences plus an honest elongation. Most published elongation values are never met in the field. The authors are quite pleased to obtain an honest 30 percent elongation for the material's life.

2. Provide a uniform level of smoothness in the substrate.

3. Achieve appropriate substrate cleaning.

4. Use multiple passes, preferably three for all installations. This will give a good level of redundancy. It is highly unlikely that workmanship errors will occur directly over each other.

5. Always require 80 dry mils minimum, with 80 to 100 more appropriate; over occupied critical areas, 120 dry mils is a good idea.

6. For exterior work, make sure the finish coat is aliphatic.

7. Do not wishful think any aspects of elastomeric.

In the next chapter, we will move from the roof of the building down to the soil for a discussion of below-grade waterproofing.

8

Below-Grade Conditions

There are two basic below-grade conditions that cover most exposures:

1. *Slab-on-ground:* This condition typically occurs at residential or low-rise structures (Figure 8-1). It is generally a slab on the ground or sometimes a sloping site that will give one side 2 to 10 feet of earth fill.

2. *Deep-below-grade construction:* Below-grade conditions, which can go down 30 to 60 feet or more.

In slab-on-ground cases, two conditions control. The first condition is where the slab-on-ground is located below grade and is within the high water table or is expected to be under rain or flood conditions. In this case, the slab needs to resist hydrostatic pressure and therefore should be treated with waterproofing.

In the second condition, the slab-on-ground is located either at grade or below grade where the high water table is a considerable distance below the slab. For this condition, the slab should receive damp-proofing, otherwise known a vapor barrier, on the positive (wet) side of the slab.

Most model building codes set the distance between the high water table and the bottom of the slab, mentioned previously, at a minimum of 6 inches below the slab. We would suggest that the design professional should request and review investigative soil reports to determine the type of soil they are dealing with and to what extent capillary rise will occur in

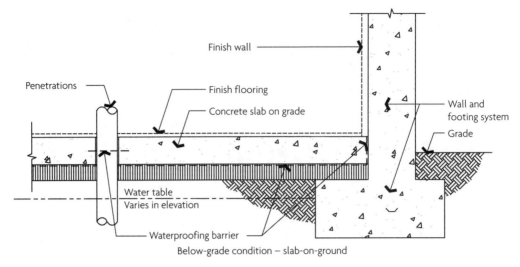

Penetrations

Finish wall

Finish flooring

Concrete slab on grade

Wall and footing system

Grade

Water table
Varies in elevation

Waterproofing barrier

Below-grade condition – slab-on-ground

Figure 8-1 A slab-on-ground condition usually used on residential and low-rise structures. *Courtesy: H. Pajo*

that type of soil. Capillary rise is the distance liquid water will rise through the soil above the water table by capillary action.

Two zones occur within the capillary rise: the saturation zone, which contains liquid water, and the zone where liquid water and vapor occur. The liquid water that occurs within the saturation zone will impose hydrostatic pressure on building slabs and walls. The depth of the saturation zone is dependent on the type of soil. Clay soil can have a saturation zone that extends over 5 feet above the table, whereas coarse sand may extend up to only 2 feet above. So even though you may have a condition where your slab is located well above the water table, depending on the type of soil on site, you may still need to provide waterproofing.

In the latter condition for slab-on-ground, where there is no hydrostatic condition or where the saturation zone is below the structure, a Class A or B vapor barrier, a 10- to 15-mil, high density, reinforced polyethylene sheet, should be used. There are many products on the market that claim to be vapor barriers but are not. We have seen manufacturers and contractors try to pass off 4- to 6-mil plastic "drop cloth" material as vapor barriers. While this product is made from polyethylene, it is low density and nonreinforced, and the perm ratings do not fall into the range set by the industry to be a vapor barrier. Because it has no reinforcement, when it is laid over gravel fill and stepped on by workers laying the steel rebar, you can imagine what will be left behind at the end of the day—Swiss cheese. In one case where a plastic sheet was used under a slab and that slab was removed years later for renovation, all that was left of the sheet were a few scattered patches of plastic—the rest had disintegrated. So make sure when you are specifying or reviewing submittals for vapor barriers that they meet the criteria as a Class A or B vapor barrier in accordance with ASTM E 1745.

For the deep-below-grade condition (Figure 8-2) and for slabs-on-ground in hydrostatic conditions, waterproofing membranes are required to stop water infiltration into the building. Waterproofing differs from damp-proofing such that waterproofing is designed to withstand hydrostatic pressures exerted upon it, whereas damp-proofing resists vapor migration through a building element. The pressures exerted can be well over 1,000 pounds per square foot in deep-below-grade conditions. We begin the discussion of below-grade waterproofing membranes next.

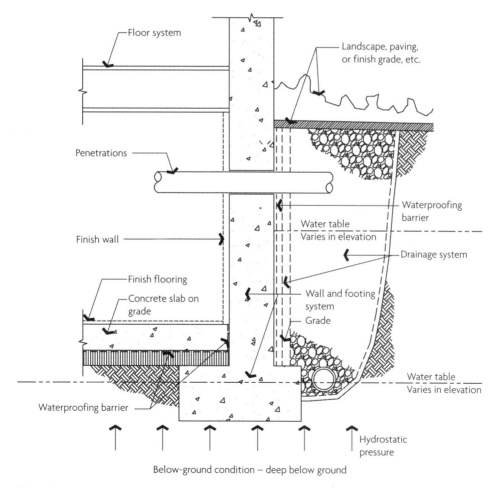

Below-ground condition – deep below ground

Figure 8-2 A wall section indicating a below-grade condition. *Courtesy: H. Pajo*

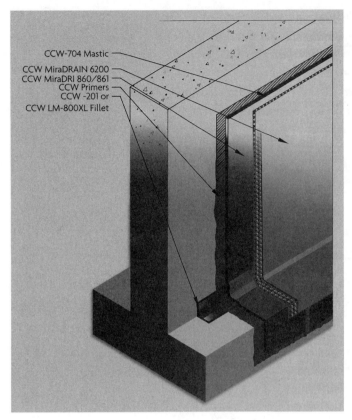

CCW-704 Mastic
CCW MiraDRAIN 6200
CCW MiraDRI 860/861
CCW Primers
CCW -201 or
CCW LM-800XL Fillet

Figure 8-3 A membrane waterproofing condition used at below-grade conditions. *Courtesy: Carlisle CCW*

MEMBRANE SYSTEMS

There is a wide variety of waterproofing membranes that are suitable for protecting subterranean work, walls, or slabs (Figure 8-3). All have their advantages and disadvantages, and some perform better in certain circumstances than others. Some of the membranes commonly used today are:

- Built-up bituminous membranes
- High-density polyethylene (HDPE) sheets
- Fluid-applied elastomeric membranes
- Self-adhering polymer-modified bitumen membranes
- Thermoplastic (polyvinyl chloride [PVC]) membranes
- Bentonite

Built-up Bituminous Membranes

Built-up waterproofing membranes were the industry-leading systems for below-grade waterproofing in the past, but have since fallen to the newer membrane systems. The biggest advantage of this system is the multiple number of plies that gives the membrane redundancy, a property that is invaluable when dealing with water infiltration. Built-up waterproofing is similar to its relative, built-up roofing, in its makeup. The two main components of the system are the organic or inorganic felts that provide the majority of reinforcement for the system, enabling it to withstand hydrostatic pressures. Organic felts have given way to inorganic felts because of the problem with organic felt's rotting over time. The second component is bitumen, which is the waterproofing and binder component of the system. There are two types of bitumens used: asphalt and coal tar pitch. Of the two, coal tar pitch offers the best performance for below-grade waterproofing.

This system is best used on jobs with large expanses of walls or slabs with minimal interruptions in the form of level of plane changes or penetrations (Figure 8-4). This type of interruption can be complicated to flash and make watertight and is one of the common causes of failure. Substrates need to have an even surface; for example, concrete substrates should not have fins, protrusions, or honeycombing.

Built-up systems are also subject to workmanship failures between plies and it becomes brittle with age and low temperatures. Because it is extremely difficult, if not impossible, to find consequential failures after installation of built-up systems, it is recommended that only built-up membranes of four plies or more be considered. They should never be solidly mopped to the substrate except at the edge conditions.

Another cause of failure in built-up systems in vertical applications is slippage. The membrane slips down the face of the substrate due to the viscosity of the bitumen used. While asphalt has a record for slippage, it is coal tar pitch that is notorious for this problem. The property of coal tar pitch known as cold flow, which gives the material its high waterproofing performance, is the culprit of the slippage. The slippage is caused by the force of gravity especially prevalent on walls in excess of 8 feet in height. Pressure caused by settling backfill is also a contributing factor to this problem. To remedy slippage, the membrane needs to be fastened at the top of the wall and back nailed every 8 feet vertically.

Figure 8-4 A completed self-adhering system on a large foundation wall. *Courtesy: Carlisle CCW*

Despite all the preceding issues mentioned, the fact is that built-up waterproofing has a long track record of performance and, as with most systems, properly installed works well. Although its use has dwindled over recent years, there are still building owners who swear by its performance.

High-Density Polyethylene (HDPE)

HDPE sheets are inexpensive and easy to work with in horizontal applications typically used below slabs or above below-grade suspended slabs.

HDPE sheets must be protected from sunlight because they will not stand up to ultraviolet exposure, and while it is resistant to many chemicals, it can degrade when exposed to certain types of acids found in soil. For this reason, it is recommended that design professionals check the soil report against the compatibility of the HDPE product they plan to specify.

Because it is thermoplastic, it tends to become brittle in low temperatures. The sheets are slick, and we have seen situations develop on the job site where a worker has easily destroyed the lap between sheets by simply walking over the membrane and squeegeeing one layer out from the other. It is a wise precaution and is typically recommended by the manufacturers to tape the joints and laps in order to avoid the laps from slipping away.

Some manufacturers even suggest mechanically fastening the laps to one another. Other methods for adhering the laps together such as heat welding are not recommended because the material will deform, creating puckers and not allowing for full adhesion. While we do not recommend using HDPE systems in cold climates, when carefully installed in warmer climates for horizontal applications, it is possible to obtain a suitable membrane. HDPE is also manufactured as films that when combined with other waterproofing material, such as bentonite, result in composite-type waterproofing systems.

Fluid-Applied Elastomeric Membranes

Fluid-applied elastomeric waterproofing—like elastomeric roofing, discussed in an earlier chapter—is available in many formulations. Unlike elastomeric roofing systems, elastomeric waterproofing systems are not resistant to ultraviolet exposure and should be covered as soon as possible. The following are some of the types typically used, but in no way are they the only systems available:

- One- and two-part urethane systems
- Rubberized asphalt systems (hot-applied)
- Modified rubber systems
- Coal-tar or asphalt-modified urethane systems

Some fluid-applied systems are installed using the hot-applied method, while others use the cold-applied method of application. Of the two types, the hot-applied systems tend to have better performance values than do their cold-applied counterparts. Typically, hot-applied systems use spunbonded polyester fabric reinforcing and can be installed in greater thicknesses than cold-applied systems, making them extremely durable, puncture resistant, and able to bridge cracks. Some cold-applied systems also use fabric reinforcement as a component of the member.

Hot-applied systems tend to cure faster, generally curing as they cool, whereas cold-applied systems can take up to 72 hours to cure. This puts hot-applied systems at an advantage because the faster curing times negate the problems inherent with cold-applied curing, such as the effects of temperature and humidity swings and the event of rain during the curing period. The biggest drawback to hot-applied systems is the requirement to have expensive jacketed kettles to heat the modified asphalt.

As mentioned previously, curing periods and consistency in cold-applied systems are an important consideration when selecting one type over the other. There are two categories in which fluid-applied membranes fall: one-component types and two-component types. Two-component membranes offer several advantages over the single-component membranes in that they have a more consistent curing period and a longer shelf life and are not as reliant on the site's humidity and temperature conditions during the curing period. It should be stressed that mixing of the components needs to be carefully and thoroughly done to specifications.

Of all the waterproofing systems, fluid-applied systems require the most stringent substrate preparations as well as strict field quality control. Substrates to which the membrane is to be applied need to be relatively dry and clean to avoid blistering, pinholing, cratering, and delamination. Concrete substrates need to be fully cured, typically 28 days, before the application of the membrane. The use of curing agents that are not compatible with the membrane system or that will not allow proper adhesion must be avoided. The concrete needs to have a wood float or steel trowel finish, and in the case of a horizontal deck, a light broom finish is recommended. Any fins or ridges protruding from the surface must be ground smooth, honeycombing needs to be filled, cracks and joints need to be filled or sealed and taped or stripped with the waterproofing manufacturer's reinforcing fabric. Most systems, if not all, require some type of primer. Weather at the time of application needs to be watched carefully because of the effects it may have on the curing; this is especially important for cold-applied systems, as mentioned above. Unlike with sheet-applied systems, which give you a consistent thickness throughout, fluid-applied system installations must be carefully monitored; it is of the utmost importance to abide by the manufacturer's application rates to achieve a consistent average thickness, especially in vertical applications. The discussion on fluid-applied membrane thickness in the previous chapter for elastomeric roofing also applies to elastomeric waterproofing. It also should be noted that the design professional needs to specify the right grade or viscosity for the type of application, either vertical or horizontal.

Because of the meticulousness of the application, these systems tend to be expensive, which must be taken into consideration when selecting the type of waterproofing system. The fact that fluid-applied waterproofing is typically self-flashing; can be applied with a roller, squeegee, brush, or trowel; and is seamless makes it the best choice for jobs with multiple penetrations and level or plane changes where sheet-type systems would be difficult to install.

GREEN NOTE

Sustainable design encourages the use of underground parking structures as a way to reduce the heat island effect of parking lots. As such, there are subsequently more below-grade structures in sustainable design. Moreover, the very nature of integrating buildings with the natural environment lends itself to buildings that follow the natural topography of a place and can lead to below-grade structures. The concepts discussed in this chapter are vital to the performance of these types of walls.

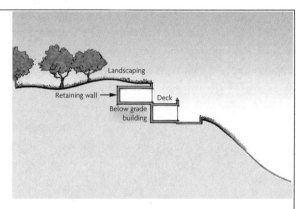

The concept section of this building shows its integration into the existing terrain. *Courtesy: C. Kaneshiro*

Bentonite Systems

Bentonite is clay developed and used by the petroleum industry to line the casing of drilling equipment. Bentonite has a very unique property: it has a very high expansion rate when it gets wet. Therefore, when it is put under compression and gets wet, it forms an impenetrable layer of clay dense enough to make a very good membrane. Its expansive properties effectively deal with almost all conditions to form a true water barrier. The authors believe it is the best below-grade membrane system to use when dealing with blindside waterproofing conditions. It is able to handle the intricacies of complicated formwork, foundation slab, and slab/wall conditions better than any other system we are aware of. It is easily handled and concrete can be poured directly on it without resulting problems inherent in other membrane materials. Bentonite waterproofing works at its optimum performance in conditions where the below-grade structure is constantly exposed to moderate to high hydrostatic pressures. When bentonite is exposed to intermittent hydrostatic pressure, the design professional must take into consideration the use of the space it will be waterproofing because bentonite that is not completely hydrated has a moderate to high vapor permeance and would not be ideal for protecting humidity- or moisture-sensitive spaces. Another caution to be aware of is in conditions where there is a constant cyclical event of hydrating and drying of the bentonite—the properties of the clay can be changed over time and may not perform as required to be a reliable waterproofing membrane. This material can be found in several waterproofing products:

- Corrugated cardboard sheets containing bentonite within the corrugations.
- Bentonite encapsulated in geo-textile mats.
- Composite systems where bentonite is laminated to HDPE sheets on one side and a water-soluble film on the other side.
- Composite systems where bentonite is laminated to polyester reinforced thermoplastic membrane sheets.
- Trowelable bentonite

Precautions must be taken, however, regarding when to use one system over the other. When using the corrugated cardboard panels, the sheet corrugation must be placed horizontally to prevent settlement of the bentonite. It should be noted that in order for the bentonite to be activated by the groundwater, the cardboard must first naturally disintegrate. During the time required for this to take place, water can infiltrate the structure before the bentonite is activated. Systems have since come out with polyethylene films or butyl coatings laminated to the panels to act as a temporary waterproofing membrane until the clay is activated. It should be protected during backfilling and should never be applied as a single layer. If panels are used, a minimum of two layers is essential for a credible installation. The joints should be staggered in both directions (Figure 8-5).

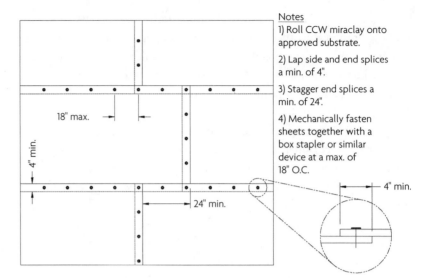

Notes

1) Roll CCW miraclay onto approved substrate.

2) Lap side and end splices a min. of 4".

3) Stagger end splices a min. of 24".

4) Mechanically fasten sheets together with a box stapler or similar device at a max. of 18" O.C.

Figure 8-5 Layout of bentonite splice conditions. *Courtesy: Carlisle CCW*

Bentonite encapsulated in geo-textile mats excels in blindside applications because the coarseness and weave of the fabric enable the mats to make a mechanical bond to the pour concrete. These mats are also ideal for below-slab waterproofing. This form of bentonite waterproofing can be specified with an HDPE film to protect the clay from premature hydration. Trowelable bentonite is used for detailed work around penetrations and corners as well as sealing gaps between lagging and sheet piling. Bentonite may also be spray applied, which makes it ideal for sheet piling conditions. The sprayed material is a bit more fragile than sheet grade. On reentrant corners, it is also best to use a cant strip in order to avoid 90-degree angles or other sharp turns. It is okay to use tube rolls of bentonite. On external corners it is also best to provide additional protection by providing a third layer over the two original two layers so that a shiplap effect is achieved. It is essential that bentonite be kept dry until all conditions of the wall or slab are complete; if not, it can fail.

Because bentonite is a clay, it is subject to root penetration if it is installed in an area where there is heavy planting. There is no problem as long as the roots are alive, as any penetrations will be sealed. If the plant dies and large roots decay and disappear, the clay material may not be able to swell sufficiently to fill in the gap. If the building is located in a saltwater tidal zone, it is essential that the bentonite be saltwater compatible. Do not rely on the manufacturer's claims regarding performance, but make sure it is properly tested for its expansion properties.

One final problem area is where bentonite approaches the ground surface. It cannot simply be taken to the surface. There will not be enough soil resistance to achieve compression. A simple solution is to coat the wall substrate with an elastomeric to 1 foot 6 inches below grade, let the bentonite lap over the elastomeric 6 inches, and then finish the backfill. Now there is a watertight grade condition (Figure 8-6).

It is our position that bentonite, properly installed, is the best below-grade protection available for a structure that is under constant hydrostatic pressure. But remember, inadequate specification or poor labor skill may destroy the system.

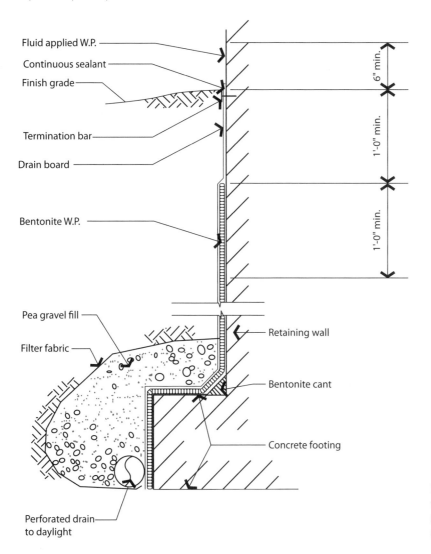

Figure 8-6 A bentonite waterproofing installation on a below-grade foundation. *Courtesy: H. Pajo*

Membrane Protection

In placing membranes against vertical subterranean walls, it is prudent to provide protection for the membrane during the construction period when workers are pursuing tasks adjacent to the membrane and while the backfill is being placed. Cases have been seen where a laborer unknowingly damaged an unprotected membrane with a hand tool or pierced it with a piece of lumber, which was being carried and accidentally swung into the membrane. A most effective protection can be gained by placing asphaltic protection sheet material, extrude polystyrene board, or high-density polyethylene drainage boards over the membrane during the construction phases or the placing of backfill. They can be left in place without any problems after the backfill is placed against them.

NEGATIVE SIDE WATERPROOFING

Application of negative side waterproofing should be considered and employed for remedial work; only rarely should one use negative side waterproofing for new construction. For below-grade problems, the best system available should be originally used because failed external membranes are unrepairable. It just isn't practical to tear up a slab or excavate 20 feet around a wall to repair a failed system. The best protection is to do a good job originally, but sometimes things do go wrong. Interior systems are difficult at best and generally expensive, but they can and will work. However, before undertaking such a system, it is wise to verify that the wall or slab is still structurally sound. This includes the rebar being intact and free from serious corrosion.

Epoxies are probably the systems that have the widest current use. They are the only systems we believe are able to develop enough of a bond to withstand a static head. They require extremely clean conditions and are touchy at best and often difficult to apply. The surface to which they are applied must also be dry and free of any dust or loose particles, although there are some products available that can be installed over damp concrete substrates. They cannot withstand any movement, as they are generally brittle when set. While it is possible to obtain some modified epoxies that are somewhat flexible, their adhesion is usually not as good as normal epoxy.

We have successfully used epoxy to a depth of approximately 30 feet with a water table head of slightly over 20 feet. In some cases, the concrete was sanded and MEK cleaned. In others, a simple MEK cleaning was adequate. Where free running water infiltration existed, the cement was chipped out to a proper shape and filled with Water Plug before the epoxy was applied. To date, the system is still working very well.

Polysulfides, strangely enough, are the only sealants we know that can be used for interior waterproofing. If the problem consists of a moving joint and does not have a large or high water head, they are the designer's best chance for success. It must be realized that they are touchy to handle and involve high labor costs. The applicator must know what he is doing; they are the best alternative to epoxy use in corrective work where movement is occurring.

The iron filling system is the oldest and is still a good system. It relies on compression under expansion to work. It is a Portland Cement mix, which employs lots of iron fillings rather than the normal stone aggregate. As the iron fillings rust, they expand and produce a very dense, compact concrete, which can form a compressive seal. To apply it correctly, cracks or stone pockets must be routed out to properly shape the sidewalls, which must be thoroughly clean. The material must have a surface it can work against in high compression. The iron filling system is not a material that can be trowel-applied to a surface and expect to get any reasonable results. It will just pop off under a direct force unless it has something to push against. Not only is it difficult to install, but also it is subject to discoloring and is very hard to paint over. It also has a tendency to bleed rust stains.

In Chapter 9, we will continue the discussion of wall systems, addressing the exterior wall finish systems.

9

Exterior Wall Systems

There are many exterior wall systems that can be employed success-fully in water infiltration–resistant design. Many systems have been around a long time, while others are relatively new. The principles are the same in that the location of the pressure differential plane is impor-tant as well as a basic understanding of the characteristics of exposure in order to know what eventual problem may arise. Generally speaking, the approach is the same for any of the materials and systems used.

In this chapter we will discuss the following exterior wall systems: Port-land cement plaster, direct-applied exterior finish systems (DEFS)/exterior insulation and finish system (EIFS) systems, concrete masonry, and metal wall systems. We will discuss curtain wall and glass in Chapter 10.

PORTLAND CEMENT PLASTER

Cement plaster is a system that has been around since the Romans first devel-oped it. In the early nineteenth century Portland cement was developed in Britain and is still the main ingredient used today in cement plaster systems and is one of the most successful wall systems on the market. There are sev-eral methods of applying cement plaster systems. The most common are:

- Three-coat systems installed over either open framing or sheathed framing with metal lath. Generally, the total thicknesses for these systems are ¾ to ⅞ inch (Figures 9-1 and 9-2).

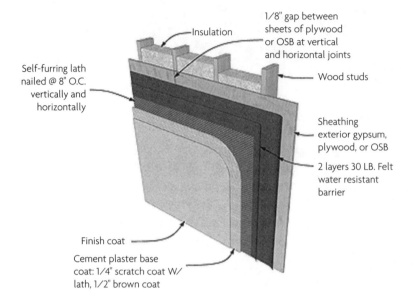

Insulation

1/8" gap between sheets of plywood or OSB at vertical and horizontal joints

Self-furring lath nailed @ 8" O.C. vertically and horizontally

Wood studs

Sheathing exterior gypsum, plywood, or OSB

2 layers 30 LB. Felt water resistant barrier

Finish coat

Cement plaster base coat: 1/4" scratch coat W/ lath, 1/2" brown coat

Figure 9-1 A three-coat plaster system applied to wood sheathing on wood stud framing system. *Courtesy: International Masonry Institute (IMI)*

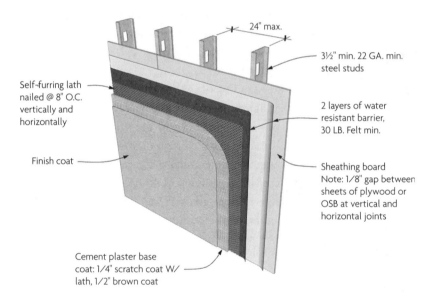

24" max.

3½" min. 22 GA. min. steel studs

Self-furring lath nailed @ 8" O.C. vertically and horizontally

2 layers of water resistant barrier, 30 LB. Felt min.

Finish coat

Sheathing board Note: 1/8" gap between sheets of plywood or OSB at vertical and horizontal joints

Cement plaster base coat: 1/4" scratch coat W/ lath, 1/2" brown coat

Figure 9-2 A three-coat plaster system applied to gypsum sheathing on metal stud framing system. *Courtesy: International Masonry Institute (IMI)*

■ Two-coat systems, commonly ⅝-inch total thickness, are installed directly over clay masonry, concrete masonry, or concrete backings (Figures 9-3, 9-4, and 9-5).

Three-Coat Plaster Systems

For the three-coat systems over metal lath, both open-framed and sheathed-framed systems perform quite well.

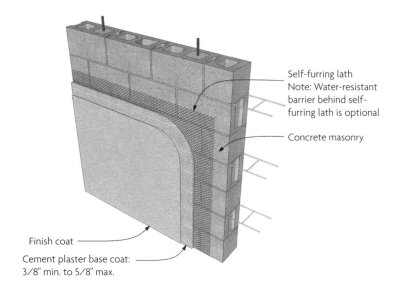

Self-furring lath
Note: Water-resistant barrier behind self-furring lath is optional

Concrete masonry

Finish coat

Cement plaster base coat: 3/8" min. to 5/8" max.

Figure 9-3 A two-coat plaster finish system on masonry wall. *Courtesy: International Masonry Institute (IMI)*

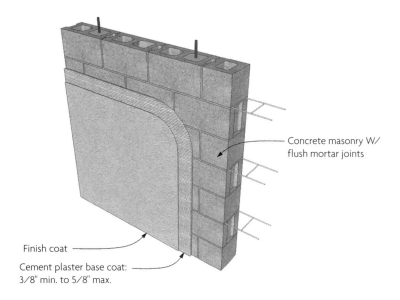

Concrete masonry W/ flush mortar joints

Finish coat

Cement plaster base coat: 3/8" min. to 5/8" max.

Figure 9-4 A direct applied plaster system on masonry wall. *Courtesy: International Masonry Institute (IMI)*

Open Framing

The lowest-cost system is the line wire system, first developed in the Los Angeles area, where it has a great track record going back several decades.

It consists of galvanized 18-gauge wire or heavier, spaced approximately 6 inches-on-center vertically, directly fastened to the exterior of the studs. The wires are then tensioned so they are "banjo string" tight.

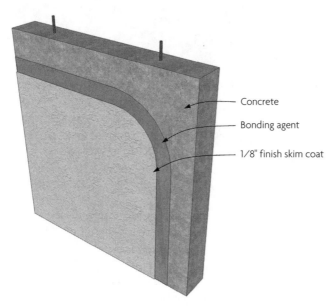

Concrete

Bonding agent

1/8" finish skim coat

Figure 9-5 A direct applied plaster system on concrete wall. *Courtesy: International Masonry Institute (IMI)*

A weather barrier consisting of either #30 building felt or paper or polymeric membrane is then fastened to the studs over the line wire properly stretched in both directions. The line wire furnishes the support for the felt membrane.

Ensure that the weather-resistive barrier properly laps the slab edge and is properly detailed at all openings. Lap weather barrier over the head flashings of openings and lap beneath sill flashings. Most important is to install the weather barriers in a shingled fashion with a minimum of 2-inch laps at horizontal joints and 6 inches for vertical joints. To protect the weather barrier from the cement plaster bonding and damaging it, either another layer of grade D building paper is added to act as a "slip" sheet or paper-backed mesh is applied over the weather-resistive barrier. Make sure the plaster, which will crack, is not bonded to the membrane and thus tear the membrane. The most important consideration that can be given to the system is that the membrane must not be damaged under any condition. An extra narrow layer of felt and mesh should be layered over all external and internal corners. In the application of either system, it is extremely critical to use nonperforated felts. If other membranes are used, ensure that their waterproofing is verified. Building paper that tends to deteriorate much faster under wet conditions should not be used.

There are critical factors to watch for in a line-wire system in order to obtain a satisfactory installation. The most important condition or area to reinforce is where the line-wire system makes a transition to solid backing such as those encountered in a shear wall of plywood or concrete masonry unit (CMU). Unless properly handled and carefully fixed, the line wire can move considerably under the action of the shear wall and result in plaster cracks or even rupture of the weather-resistive barrier membrane at the joint. Another concern of the system is that the line wires be stretched so they do not stretch or sag to the extent that a variation in the thickness of plaster will occur, which can lead to additional cracking or other undesirable situations.

Available today are many varieties of polymeric membranes, also known as weather-resistive barriers (WRBs), designed to be used behind Portland cement plaster systems. We have found some to work, while others seem dubious. We have found grade D, #30 building paper to be tried and true, although in instances where air infiltration is an issue—which seems to be the case in today's constructions practices—as well as durability, the architect will then need to carefully select a membrane that will resist water and air from infiltrating the wall from the outside, while still allowing water vapor to escape from the interior. This type of membrane is known as a vapor-permeable WRB.

- Sheet-type polymeric membranes are made from several types of polyolefins; polyethylene or polypropylene woven, nonwoven or spunbonded.
- Fluid-applied WRBs are water based; fabric-reinforced latex membranes typically are used in EIFS and are usually a proprietary product from the EIFS manufacture.
- Typically, these WRBs are tested per ASTM D 779 for water resistance, the same procedure used to test building paper. This test is known to fail some of the polymeric membranes because of their water vapor permeability and basically giving false results as to their water resistance. For these types of membranes, the architect should require that the membrane be tested per AATCC 127, Water Resistance: Hydrostatic Pressure Test, because it gives a more accurate result as to the water resistance of the membrane.

For vapor permeability the membrane should be tested per ASTM E 96 Method B.

By taking all necessary precautions in plaster wall application, all three problems can be avoided and an acceptable, watertight exterior wall system will result.

Sheathed Framing

The second system relies on a solid backing, such as plywood, oriented strand board (OSB), exterior glass-mat-faced gypsum board, lumber sheathing, or insulation weather board, to take the pressure exerted upon the application of the various plaster coats. In such a system, if using building paper or felt for your weather-resistive barrier, it is perfectly acceptable to use two layers of #15 felt as a minimum, because the solid backing will provide enough support to the lighter-weight membrane. We prefer to use a vapor-permeable polymeric weather-resistive barrier over the sheathing followed by the metal lath that is backed with type I, grade D building paper. The installation of the weather-resistive barrier is similar to that of the open framing system discussed earlier. It is important in this type of a system to avoid large gaps or cracks in the substrate for obvious reasons.

In either three-coat system, lath reinforcement is required for the application of the plaster. There are three types of metal lath most commonly used:

- Expanded metal lath
- Woven wire mesh
- Welded wire mesh

The openings in the mesh should not exceed 4 square inches in order for the plaster to properly key into the mesh. It is strongly recommended that no matter which type of lath you specify, it should be galvanized in a hot-dipped process, and it should have a G-60 coating in accordance to ASTM A653. The galvanizing process should be done after the fabrication of the lath to ensure that all exposed surfaces receive the coating and that the coating doesn't chip or flake off during fabrication.

Expanded metal lath is fabricated from steel coils that are slit to form the diamond-shaped openings when the metal is expanded. Expanded metal lath comes in several forms—self-furred, flat, or rib style—and several weights—1.75, 2.5, or 3.4 lb/square yard, depending on the gauge of the steel coil used. The greater the weight, the stiffer the lath is. The architect should refer to the PCA Portland Cement Plaster/Stucco manual as to what style and weight of expanded metal lath to use for a particular application (Figure 9-6).

Woven wire mesh lath is fabricated from galvanized steel wire using the reverse twist method to form the hexagonal openings in the mesh. Woven wire lath is available as flat or self-furring, paper backed, and with stiffener wire backing. For mesh openings of 1 inch, 1½-inches, and 2 inches, 20-, 17-, and 16-gauge wire, respectively, is used (Figure 9-7).

Welded wire mesh lath comes in flat and self-furring, with and without paper backing, fabricated from ASTM A 641 cold-drawn galvanized steel wire. The wires are run vertically and horizontally, with a spacing of no more than 2 inches and welded to

Figure 9-6 Metal lath used for plaster wall systems. *Courtesy: H. Pajo*

each other at each intersection to form the mesh. A 14-gauge stiffener wire is added at a spacing of 6 inches on center running parallel to the long dimension of the mesh sheet.

When installing the metal lath, it must be stretched tight and taut. A double stretch, which is applied in both directions, will provide better reinforcing under stressed conditions to keep the plaster from excessive cracking. Four-inch laps should occur at all edges. All reentrant corners should have a double lath applied for a distance of 9 inches in both directions. No laps should occur within one foot of any corner and the lath must be uniformly furred. As mentioned earlier, use a slip sheet or paper-backed lath over the membrane. Care must be taken when lapping paper-backed lath, in that the paper must always lap the paper

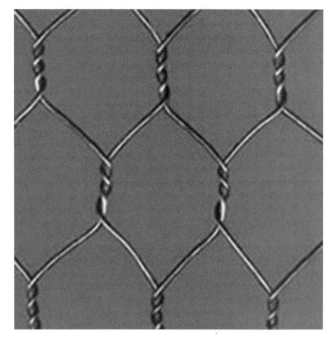

Figure 9-7 Woven-type wire mesh. *Courtesy: H. Pajo*

of the next sheet of lath and not get placed between the sheets of metal lath, as this will interfere with the bond between the two sheets of metal lath and can cause major cracking at that point.

If expansion joints (Figure 9-8) are used, the lath must terminated at or be cut out behind the joint and wire tied to the flange of the expansion joint accessory. More often than not, this procedure is not performed correctly because it is labor intensive; however, if not done properly, the value of the expansion joint would be compromised, defeating its purpose. So when inspecting the work in the field, be sure to inspect these types of joints closely.

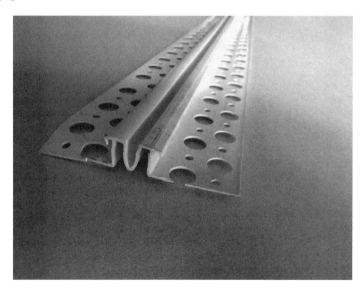

Figure 9-8 A plaster expansion joint. *Courtesy: H. Pajo*

Foundation weep screeds (Figures 9-9, 9-10, and 9-11) are an absolute must for all sill conditions and at endwall and sidewall roof conditions, as

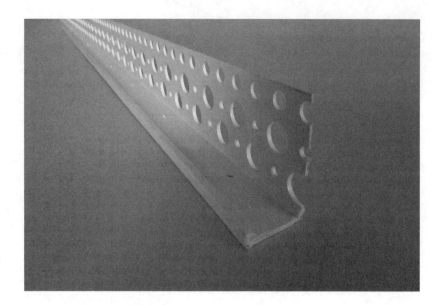

Figure 9-9 A vinyl weep screed used at plaster wall bottom termination. *Courtesy: H. Pajo*

Interior

Exterior

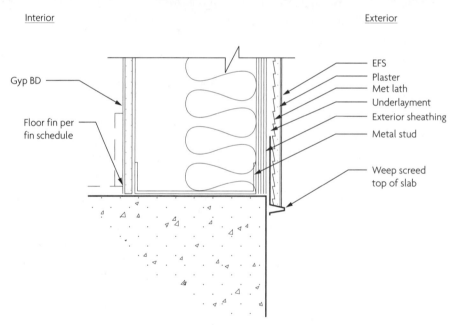

Gyp BD

Floor fin per fin schedule

EFS
Plaster
Met lath
Underlayment
Exterior sheathing
Metal stud

Weep screed top of slab

Figure 9-10 Plaster weep screed used at bottom of wall terminations. *Courtesy: H. Pajo*

well as at head flashing conditions for wall openings. When using weep screeds, a common mistake in the field is to apply sealant along the bottom edge with a large bead, thus covering the weep holes. This can prove to be detrimental to the wall system, allowing water to collect and back up

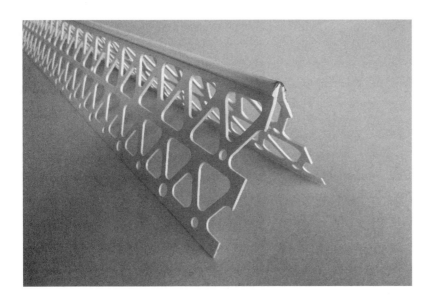

Figure 9-11 A vinyl corner bead used at plaster corner conditions. *Courtesy: H. Pajo*

behind the cement plaster, not letting it dry out and causing the metal lath and screed to rust. Make sure to check these conditions when doing your field walk-through.

Two-Coat Plaster Systems

Two-coat Portland cement plaster systems are typically applied over solid concrete cementitious or clay masonry bases that when properly prepared need not require lath or mesh reinforcement. Concrete bases need to be properly cured and free from laitance, form release oils and agents, or curing compounds. If not properly cured, the concrete will have the tendency to absorb the water from the plaster mix at an accelerated rate, thus causing the plaster to dry faster than required to set properly, leading to cracking, shrinking, and debonding from the substrate. Check that concrete walls are true in line and plane and free of voids, honeycombing, and concrete fins, and repair surface defects as required to receive the plaster finish.

For existing concrete, the substrate should be examined for misalignment, cracks, voids, or other surface defects that need to be addressed prior to the application of the plaster. Any coatings such as paint, waterproofing, or repellants, oils, or other material affecting the bond between the plaster and substrate should be removed and cleaned. These coatings can be removed by light sandblasting or with high-pressure water spray. The absorption rate of the prepared surface should then be tested to see whether the plaster can be directly applied to the concrete or if a bonding agent or lath is required prior to the plaster application.

When applying Portland cement plaster to a concrete masonry base, similar guidelines for preparing concrete bases for plaster should be practiced. As a rule of thumb, one should specify using open-textured CMU for walls to receive cement plaster because the porous nature of the surface provides excellent keying for the plaster to bond to the substrate. The mortar joints should be specified to be cut flush to aid in lessening the telegraphing of the joints through the plaster finish. Tooling or floating the joints is not recommended, as the excess mortar is floated over the surface of the masonry, which negatively affects the bond between the plaster and concrete masonry. Lightly wetting the surface of the concrete masonry base is recommended to control differential suction between the masonry unit and the mortar joints. This is necessary in controlling the joint patterning from "ghosting" through the two-coat plaster finish. Similar precautions apply to clay masonry as well. For glazed or hard dense brick, the surface should be scored or abraded prior to receiving the plaster finish. If in examining the brick substrate it is found to be sound structurally but the surface is disintegrated to the point where there can be no sufficient bond, then lath reinforcement needs to be used.

Plaster Mixes

Not only is the application of plaster finish important, but the mix of the plaster is equally fundamental. A poor and improper mix will produce an inferior plaster job, which in itself will be responsible for all types of water infiltration problems.

Type II cement mixes should be used in all conditions, with one half Portland cement and one half plastic cement. Under no conditions should lime, clay, or any other ingredients be used for mixes in exterior plaster applications. Any sand to be used should be #2, washed and graded with four to five parts sand to one part cement for the scratch and brown coats. In the scratch and brown coat, it is advisable to add polypropylene or alkali-resistant glass fiber to the mix. Water is then added to achieve a 2½-inch maximum slump. It should be noted that the slump is for plaster cones that are only 6 inches tall.

Portland cement plaster should never be worked in temperatures above 80°Fahrenheit or those below 40°. The scratch ⅜-inch-thick coat must be well keyed with extreme care not to rip the membrane during its application. In lieu of following the provisions of the building code, which call for a minimum of 24 hours between first and second coats [International Building Code Table 2512.6], it is desirable to double up on the brown coat, also ⅜ inch thick, within 12 hours in spite of code provisions. The final coat should be applied to create a full ⅞-inch plaster thickness and as long as possible after the brown coat. If over two days have elapsed, pressure wash the plaster. In climates with hot ambient temperatures and in dry and windy conditions, coats should be fog sprayed continuously for a minimum of 72 hours, and an additional 12 hours of fog spraying should occur for each day in which the temperature exceeds 80 Fahrenheit. If the plaster dries out too rapidly, it might as well be removed and applied over again from scratch. An additional period of 14 days of dry curing should be allowed, if possible, prior to the final coat. The longer the curing time, the more shrinkage will be stabilized and the easier to correct shrinkage cracks in the brown coat.

EXTERIOR INSULATION FINISH SYSTEMS (EIFS)

Developed in Europe in the 1950s and first introduced to North America in the 1970s, EIFS has become a widely used wall-cladding system across Canada and the United States. The basic EIFS is comprised of multiple components, which include expanded polystyrene insulation board, mechanical fasteners or adhesives to secure the insulation board to the wall substrate, and a lamina that in itself is made up of several components. Laminas typically consist of a base coat, glass fiber reinforcing mesh, and a finish coat that contains the color and texture for the finished appearance. While this basic material has been used extensively and successfully in Europe, one should remember that in Europe it is almost exclusively applied over masonry type walls. In the United States the system is installed over many types of walls, including stick framing, concrete, and concrete masonry, to name a few. In stick-framed construction, the substrate to which the EIFS is applied can be exterior-grade plywood, glass-mat-faced exterior gypsum board, or, in some systems, cement backer boards. EIFS falls into two classifications, the first being polymer based (PB) and the second polymer modified (PM), also known in the industry as "soft coat" and "hard coat," respectively. The polymer-based system is the most commonly specified system today; however, some still use the polymer-modified system where impact resistance is paramount.

Water management for EIFS is the major concern for architects and engineers, especially in lieu of all the litigation cases that occurred in the 1990s with EIFS. These systems are known as face-sealed systems that depend on the exterior face and single-stage seals to resist water infiltration. In most of these systems the actual membrane is usually under 10 mils thick. It is also worth noting that in independent testing these systems usually leak. This system is definitely not recommended in any climate that sees moderate to heavy rainfall. In these systems there is no secondary line of defense, and if not maintained or installed properly, especially at joints, openings, and interfaces with other building envelope components, the result can prove disastrous. While the failures that drove the legal action in the 1990s were attributed to workmanship and lack of flashings at openings, it spurred on manufacturers to develop systems to better manage water that will undoubtedly get past the exterior face of the wall system. The results were three systems frequently used today: a dual-barrier system, a drained system, and a drained pressure-moderated system sometimes referred to as a rain screen EIFS.

Dual-Barrier Systems

The dual-barrier system (Figure 9-12) has two lines of defense against water infiltration, the first being again the exterior skin or lamina. The

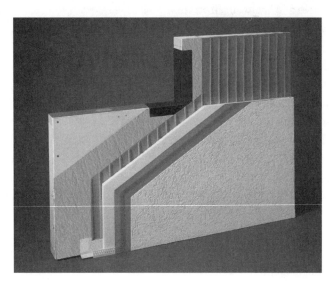

secondary barrier, a membrane known as a weather-resistive barrier (see sidebar on WRBs), is either a fluid-applied membrane or a sheet membrane that is placed over the substrate and behind the insulation board. At the joints there is a two-stage sealant system that creates a drainage channel in the joint that allows water that gets past the exterior to drain down and out. In multi-story buildings, weep tubes are installed in the vertical joints at intervals to allow water to escape to the outside, mitigating the buildup of water pressure that can occur in the heights of these type of structures. This system, while having a secondary barrier to prevent water infiltration, does not offer

Figure 9-12 A dual-barrier EIFS system. *Courtesy: Dryvit Systems, Inc.*

drainage at that barrier. So in buildings with this system in locations that see heavy rainfall, there is the potential for moisture to penetrate.

Drained Systems

Drained systems are very similar to dual-barrier systems in that they are comprised of similar components but differ in that they have a drainage layer between the insulation board and the WRB. This drainage layer can be formed in several methods, one of which is to place geotextile sheets or plastic drainage mats over the WRB prior to installing the insulation board. Another method is to create drainage channels behind the insulation board by troweling the insulation adhesive in vertical ribbons or by using insulation boards that have vertical grooves routed in the back of the boards. As to which method to use, it is typically dependant on which EIFS manufacturer is selected. The advantage of this system is obvious in that it won't allow moisture or water to accumulate between the substrate and the insulation board and allows the wall system to dry out. This water drainage can be adversely affected by the introduction of wind pressure acting upon the building, thus the development of the last system to be talked about.

Drained Pressure-Moderated System

In a nutshell, this system works off the model of the rain screen principal in which specifically sized, compartmentalized cavities are located between the wall substrate and the exterior insulation layer. These cavities, along with calculated numbers of vent openings strategically located in the joints of the finish system, work together to create an equalization of pressure within the drainage plane, thus controlling and minimizing the amount of rainwater that gets into the cavities (Figure 9-13). This becomes an important factor, especially in windy and wet weather conditions where the winds can create nonuniform pressure differentials across the face of a building. By compartmentalizing the cavities and creating smaller individual volumes of air,

Figure 9-13 A drained pressure-moderated EIFS system. *Courtesy: Dryvit Systems, Inc.*

it becomes possible to control the ever-changing pressure differential acting on the build skin, whereas in noncompartmental designs such as the previous system mentioned, it is not possible to have pressure equalization. Some systems, if designed properly, can actually prevent water from getting into the cavities.

The drawback to these wall systems is that they require a high degree of design and engineering as well as high-quality workmanship in order for them to work properly, which usually means that they are expensive. The slightest deviations in the design can enormously affect the performance. Proper sizing of the vent holes depends on the volume of the compartment it serves, the airtightness of the WRB or air barrier, and the rigidity of the exterior and interior layers.

Direct-Applied Exterior Finish System

Direct-applied exterior finish systems (DEFSs) are wall systems that derive from EIFSs. This system is basically the finish lamina and reinforcement applied directly to the wall substrate with no insulation board. We tend to use this system over concrete, concrete masonry walls, or cement plaster substrates and do not recommend using them directly over exterior-type gypsum board of plywood substrates, especially in climates with moderate to heavy rainfall, because they fall into the category of face-sealed systems or single-line barrier walls, which, as discussed earlier, rely on only one line of defense against water infiltration.

Design Considerations

In choosing the type of system that suits the project, the design professional must take into account several factors, including climate conditions, building orientation and wall exposure, types of substrates used, level of impact resistance at areas within reach of people's touch, maintenance equipment, automobiles, and so on. In these areas, one may want to use the polymer modified coat system or the polymer-based system, using reinforcing mesh rated for high impact in those obtainable regions. A major point of failure in EIFSs is where they interface with other building envelope systems, for example, window and door openings and sidewall conditions at roofs. These areas should be detailed very carefully with the proper flashings. Back-wrapping the mesh around exposed edges of the insulation boards is of the utmost importance to avoid failures at the joints and terminations. EIFS accessories such as casing beads and foundation screeds,

GREEN NOTE

Material specifications in sustainable design emphasize reducing, reusing, and recycling our natural resources. Project goals typically are aimed toward maximizing the percentages of recycled materials, reused or salvaged materials, regionally harvested materials, woods from certifiable sustainable forests, and rapidly renewable materials. While most of these products are produced by manufacturers who provide material data sheets and warranty information, architects should be careful about the use of reused materials, especially in new assemblies. Since these products are commonly salvaged from other job sites, they do not carry a manufacturer's warranty and could void another product's warranty if used in an assembly, for example, a wall system. If the salvaged product is used as a veneer where it is not the main water infiltration protection, then this is a more acceptable solution.

The rock veneer was salvaged from another location, cleaned, and reused as veneer material on this wall. The water infiltration protection is provided by the wall assembly, which supports the rock veneer. *Courtesy: C. Kaneshiro*

as with cement plaster systems, need to be installed properly. Placement of sealant needs to be scrutinized; we have seen sealant being applied to the underside of foundation weep screeds where the sealant bead was so large that it covered the weep holes of the accessories, rendering it pretty much useless. Luckily, this was caught during a quality assurance mock-up and remedied before the installation of the actually wall. We have also seen cases were the sealants were not bonded to the base coat but instead to the finish coat. Sealants must be bonded to the base coat in order to obtain the adhesion necessary to remain intact during the stress and strain of movement. Adhesion can fail when sealant is applied to the finish coat because the additives in the finish used to prohibit moisture absorption will not allow the sealant to bond correctly. Other sealant properties come into play as well, such as joint size and sealant shape, compatibility with the base-coat materials, and the use of primers, many of which will be discussed in Chapter 11.

All in all, the exterior insulated finish systems used today can prove to be high-performance-type wall systems, provided that the design considerations are strictly taken into account, that there is a good-quality assurance program put into force, and that a highly qualified contractor with experience in installing these systems is employed. There is no reason why one should not expect a leak-free system for several years. Ultimately, though, it is up to the architect or design professional to clearly understand the product's strengths and limitations and to make sure all the criteria are specified in the contract documents.

MASONRY WALLS

Masonry construction systems include glass block (Figure 9-14), concrete masonry units (CMUs; Figures 9-15 and 9-16), brick, cut stone, and cement rubble masonry (CRM; Figure 9-17) walls. By their nature, masonry walls give the appearance of strength, and rightfully so—the structural integrity of the material makes it one of the most durable of wall materials. The fact that Roman masonry walls (Figure 9-18) can still be seen in Europe is a testament to this fact.

Figure 9-14 A glass block component that is usually grouted together into a wall system. *Courtesy: H. Pajo*

However, masonry is not exempt from water infiltration and care still must be taken in correctly waterproofing these systems. It may be a surprise to some, but CMU and typical brick walls are pervious to moisture. Stone, CRM, and glass block tend to be less pervious materials.

Waterproofing is especially important in masonry systems, which employ steel reinforcing. Steel reinforcing (Figure 9-19) provides CMU walls with greater strength and allows for increased heights. If water were to penetrate the surface and reach the steel, it would corrode the reinforcing and undermine the structural integrity of the wall.

Figure 9-15 A concrete masonry unit (CMU). *Courtesy: H. Pajo*

For above-ground masonry walls, two types of systems typically accomplish water-proofing:

1. Surface water repellents
2. Integral water repellents

Surface water repellents are applied to the exterior face of the masonry wall after construction. This type of repellent should allow vapor transmission to allow moisture interior to the wall to escape. Otherwise, there is a potential for blistering and peeling to occur when moisture builds up under the exterior coating. When choosing a water repellent product, it is important that the product is able to resist the alkalin-

Figure 9-16 A completed CMU wall system awaiting an exterior finish. *Courtesy: H. Pajo*

ity of fresh mortar. Alternatively, you can apply a fill coat to the wall prior to applying the water repellent.

Integral water repellents are incorporated into the masonry material before wall construction. Typically, this repellent is an admixture, which is added to the concrete mix at the CMU plant. Theoretically, each block has water resistance built in. Be sure that the mortar mix also has an integral water repellent admixture. The use of other concrete admixtures in

Figure 9-17 A masonry rubble composite wall system. *Courtesy: H. Pajo*

combination with water repellent additives is not recommended. It is important also to note that integral water repellents are soluble if immersed in water for long periods of time. Therefore, mortar joints should be tooled, not raked, and high-pressure water cleaning should be avoided.

Specific surface water repellent treatments include the following:

- *Cementitious coatings.* Discussed earlier in this chapter, stucco or cement plaster systems are an excellent choice for masonry walls. They can provide aesthetic texture and color choices.

- *Paint:*
  - *Fill coats.* Used to fill voids, smooth irregularities, or provide a base separation from the alkali reactions, these products are commonly made from latex coatings and Portland cement.
  - *Cement-based paints.* These products contain Portland cement as a binder. As such, they are not subject to reaction with the alkali mortar.
  - *Latex paints.* These water-based coatings are resistant to alkali by nature, are durable, and allow for vapor transmission.
  - *Alkyd paints.* A low-cost alternative, these products also have low alkali resistance and must be used carefully as a masonry water repellent. You could consider using this product in combination with a fill coat.

- *Clear treatments:*
  - *Silicone resins.* These are the most widely used silicone-based water repellents for masonry. They penetrate masonry surfaces easily and are excellent at repelling water. However, they need to be applied to air-dry surfaces.
  - *Silanes.* Similar to silicone resin, this product can be applied to slightly damp surfaces.
  - *Siloxances.* These have all the benefits of silanes but they have a wider range of surface acceptance than silanes. Cost for this product tends to be higher.

■ *Acrylics.* Providing an elastic film over the masonry wall as a barrier to moisture, acrylics are similar to silicone resins in cost and also need to be applied on dry surfaces.

Some epoxy-, rubber-, and oil-based paints claim to provide exterior water repellent treatment for masonry. However, these coatings do not allow the wall to breathe, and as such they can blister or peel if water moisture builds up behind them.

Masonry cavity walls (Figure 9-20) consist of an inner structural masonry wall, called a wythe, and an outer wythe, with an air cavity between them. The wythes do not need to be constructed of the same material. In this type of construction the cavity typically acts as the waterproof system. As long as no "bridges" exist for water to cross from outer to inner wythe, the cavity will collect moisture before reaching the inner surface. As such, waterproofing coatings are only necessary where there is "bridging," other potential sources of water (like roof conditions), or the decision to provide additional moisture protection.

Figure 9-18 Ancient Roman wall system standing the test of time. *Courtesy: M. Eriksson*

Any of the surface water repellents can be used to treat the outer surface of the inner wythe in a cavity wall. Because it is not visible, the appearance of the inner wythe is not a vital issue.

The bottom of the cavity must be detailed properly to allow water, which has passed through the outer wythe, to exit. Continuous flashing and weep holes along the bottom are the typical solution.

Composite walls are another standard wall system seen with masonry. They consist of an inner and an outer wall structure adjacent to one another, similar to a cavity wall without the cavity (Figure 9-21). The wall materials are typically different. For example, the designer could combine

Figure 9-19 Steel reinforcement protruding from CMU. Once walls are completed and solid grouted, the wall will have the required strength. *Courtesy: Jason T. Coleman*

stone veneer on CMU, brick over concrete, and even CRM over plywood on metal stud. The important thing to remember is to waterproof the exterior-facing surface of the inner wall structure and be sure to have an exit path for the water at the base such as the weeps and flashing described earlier.

METAL WALL SYSTEMS

Metal wall systems (Figure 9-22) are basically exterior wall cladding comprised of typically aluminum but also can be steel, stainless steel, copper, titanium, and other composite materials. These systems have been around for more than 30 years and have become commonplace applications as rectilinear preengineered buildings (Figure 9-23).

However, in the past decade, metal wall systems have become the cladding of choice for contemporary designers such as Frank Gehry and Daniel Libeskind. Technology and computerized manufacturing allowed these systems to be utilized in ways previously unimaginable or at least unconstructable. It is not untypical for each cladding component on these structures to be unique. In other words, each piece of metal is custom fabricated or one of a kind. When there are thousands of such pieces, you can only begin to imagine the construction challenge, including the waterproofing question.

The following types of metal panel systems are available:

- *Lap-seam metal panels.* Formed from 0.05-inch-thick metal sheets, these panels are typically ship-lapped and come in strips of up to 4 feet wide and 20 feet long. Gutters or sealant tape are typically applied along their edges.

- *Composite metal wall panels.* These panels consists of two sheets of metal adhered to a core material. The overall panel thickness varies

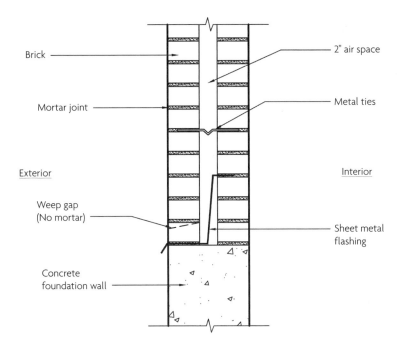

Brick

2" air space

Mortar joint

Metal ties

Exterior

Interior

Weep gap
(No mortar)

Sheet metal
flashing

Concrete
foundation wall

Figure 9-20 A cross-section
detailing of a cavity wall with a
flashing to direct water to the
outside of wall. *Courtesy: H. Pajo*

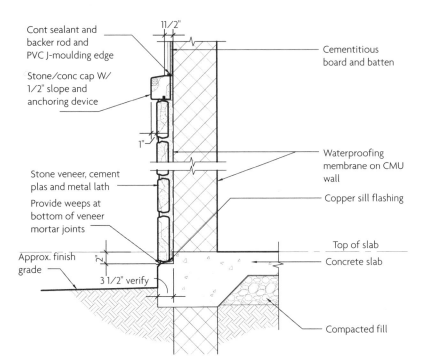

Cont sealant and
backer rod and
PVC J-moulding edge

11/2"

Cementitious
board and batten

Stone/conc cap W/
1/2" slope and
anchoring device

1"

Waterproofing
membrane on CMU
wall

Stone veneer, cement
plas and metal lath

Provide weeps at
bottom of veneer
mortar joints

Copper sill flashing

Approx. finish
grade

2"

Top of slab

Concrete slab

3 1/2" verify

Compacted fill

Figure 9-21 A cross-section
of a masonry composite wall
system. Emphasis here is to
drain the moisture to the outside
of the wall. *Courtesy: H. Pajo*

Figure 9-22 Disney Hall in Los Angeles, California, uses a metal wall panel system. *Courtesy: C. Kaneshiro*

from 1.2 inch to over 2 inches, depending on the insulation. The metal sheets are typically 0.05 inches in thickness. Composite metal wall panels are often ship-lapped with adjacent panels but provide greater strength than lap-seamed installations. The core can be foam or honeycomb insulation (Figures 9-24, 9-25 and 9-26).

■ *Metal-faced composite panels.* Similar to the composite panel, the metal-faced composite panel consists of thin (0.05 inches) metal facings attached to a thin (up to ¼-inch thick) thermoplastic core. The resulting composite panel is then bent to the desired profile. These panels are not as impact resistant as flat plate; however, depending on the size of the panels, stiffeners can be welded or adhered to the rear surface of the panels. The size of metal-faced composite panels is generally less than 10 feet by 10 feet. These panels are generally fastened by proprietary installation systems.

■ *Flat plate metal wall panels.* Fabricated typically from ⅛- inch-thick metal plates, these panels are stronger than other types of metal systems and have a high impact resistance and durability. Panels can be shaped and bent into different profiles. Stiffeners and supports are sometimes welded or adhered to the flat plate. The thickness of the system depends on the structural support system for the panels. Size and span of the panel are directly proportional to the thickness of the system. Panels can be attached directly to the structural system or to a secondary structural system.

There is a wide variety of waterproofing systems used for metal panel systems, including:

■ *Face-sealed barrier systems.* These systems rely on the exterior skin of the cladding to provide the water-resistant barrier. Since metal by nature is not pervious, the critical components of face-sealed barrier systems are the joints. Thermal and differential movement must be accounted for in the design. Metal has a considerable thermal coefficient of expansion. Sealants must be able to handle the dimensional changes at joints, which will be influenced by the type of metal and also climatic temperature change. Moreover, other climatic factors that need to be considered include ultraviolet exposure, wind patterns, and salt-air composition, to name a few. The bottom line for face-sealed barrier systems is that the system is only as good as the sealant selected. Failure of the sealant will esult in failure of the system and a potential liability for owner and designer.

Figure 9-23 A composite wall panel system used on modern buildings. *Courtesy: Alucobond (Division of Alcan)*

■ *Weeped drainage systems.* Drainage systems are designed to direct and channel water away from the exterior façade to stormwater conveyance points. These systems do not rely on sealants as a barrier to moisture; rather, the joints are unsealed to allow water into the system. As in face-sealed barriers, sources of movement must be considered in the system design.

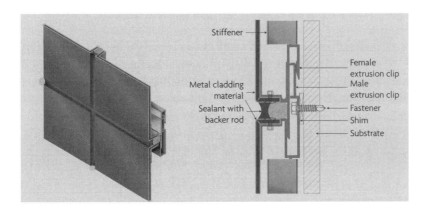

Figure 9-24 A composite wall panel—wet seal joint system. *Courtesy: Alucobond (Division of Alcan)*

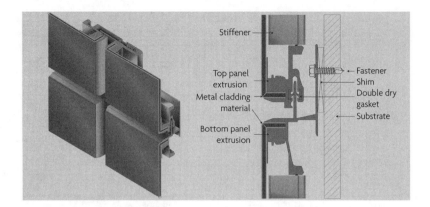

Figure 9-25 A composite wall panel—dry seal joint system. *Courtesy: Alucobond (Division of Alcan)*

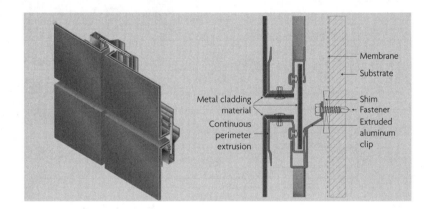

Figure 9-26 A composite wall panel—rain screen system. *Courtesy: Alucobond (Division of Alcan)*

■ *Rain screens.* When used as rain screens, metal wall systems are totally dependent on water-resistant barriers on a secondary skin behind them. The metal systems are decorative façades that provide a canvas for artistic expression and shading. The secondary skin can be composed of any number of solutions we have already discussed, depending on the structure and design of the building.

Simpler metal panel systems tend to be barrier systems and weeped drainage systems. Complex structures like those of Frank Gehry typically use rain screen systems. The decorative metal panels may shed water, but the building's primary water infiltration protection comes from behind the exterior skin. Obviously, the owner pays a premium for these types of systems, but there is a satisfaction of creating structures never before thought possible.

10

Metal and Glass Curtain Walls

METAL AND GLASS CURTAIN WALL SYSTEMS

Basically, there are two common methods of fabrication/installation of metal and glass curtain walls, which are used in the exterior treatment of buildings (Figure 10-1):

- The stick system
- The unitized panel system (Figures 10-2, 10-3, and 10-4)

Stick System

The stick system is made up of individual extruded pieces of metal. They are generally delivered to the job site in packages of running lengths and are field erected. Erection requires that the components be screwed together or, rarely, bolted together, except when they are fastened directly to the building in fixed connections. Some older methods not commonly used today involved stapling or dovetailing the frame members together. This system tends to be more flexible in its installation because placement of the framing members need not be sequential, allowing work to be performed both horizontally and vertically over the building and at different locations simultaneously. Even with this flexibility, quality construction practices and methods call for some order in the installation of components.

The biggest issue with stick system fabrications is how to deal with lateral movement (seismic and building sway) and vertical movement

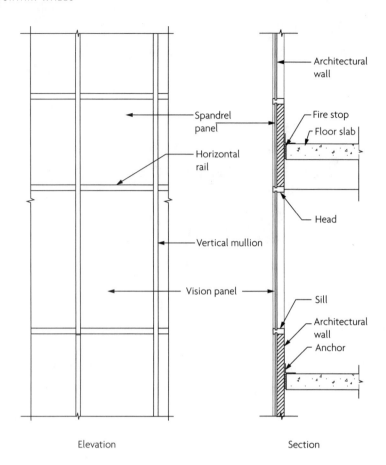

Architectural
wall

Spandrel
panel

Fire stop

Floor slab

Horizontal
rail

Head

Vertical mullion

Vision panel

Sill

Architectural
wall

Anchor

Elevation

Section

Figure 10-1 Drawing calling out basic component terminology. *Courtesy: H. Pajo*

(seismic and slab deflection) within the building as well as thermal expansion and contraction. Stick systems are impacted more by these types of movement because the components are field assembled, limiting quality control of the fabrication of the system. In fact, by the nature of their installation, stick systems are limited to small amounts of lateral movement and sway. Vertical mullions typically span across two floors and require spliced joints at those intervals. These mullions are anchored at each floor, and then the horizontal mullions are installed in between. With the verticals anchored at each floor, the system more than likely can handle the movement differential from one floor to the next. However, when the amount of displacement is compounded over the entire building, for example, in a high-rise structure, the tendency for this system is to twist and rack, opening the joints at the horizontal to vertical mullion connection and at the splices, making the curtain wall susceptible to water infiltration. For this reason we would recommend this type of installation only for low-rise buildings, where seismic movement and building sway across the entire structure is minimal compared to a midrise or high-rise structure.

Thermal expansion is another type of movement the architects need to be aware of, and more often than not it is neglected. The most common metal used today for the framing members is aluminum, which touts the highest coefficient of thermal expansion, and for every 100°F rise in temperature and 10-foot-long mullion can elongate to one-eighth of an inch. This is a large amount and, if not designed for, can cause big headaches for everyone. For example, if you have a building that measures 150 feet across its face with metal curtain

Figure 10-2 Curtain wall unitized system being installed on a midrise building. *Courtesy: Arcadia*

wall divided into 4-foot increments, each of the horizontal strips of metal is 4 feet long and is butt-jointed to a vertical member. In terms of expansion of the metal pieces, it is more realistic to look at the amount of expansion accrued over 150 feet than that incurred over a 4-foot length. The real meaning, in terms of expansion, is that for every one of the 4-foot sticks, if and when they are tight fitted to the vertical mullions—which is seldom the case—they all become hot from exposure to direct sun. As such, there will be an outward expansion, which will result in some deformation on the metal. Upon cooling, the metal pieces will contract and the joints will open up to water infiltration. There is no way these joints can be made tight after deformation occurs. If there is no deformation, it means the metal-to-metal joints were not tight in the beginning and thus, after a few months, also generally means water infiltration.

It is possible, however, to make a stick system fairly effective if the horizontals are run through continuously and verticals fastened to them. This makes gravity work on behalf of the system wherein the weight of the metal sticks will press into the joint and reduce its exposure. In addition,

Figure 10-3 A partially completed storefront system utilizing the unitized system. *Courtesy: Arcadia*

it also becomes possible to collect any water that has infiltrated the joint and get it out. Systems that have adopted such a fabrication technique have proven to be most effective. We believe the only problem is to make sure there is some allowance for thermal expansion or the wall will walk off the building. But this is a surmountable situation.

Usually, when the vertical members are run through, which is apparently what every architect seems to want for aesthetic considerations, water infiltration problems will arise. The other fact is that when the verticals run through, invariably to make erection procedures easier and fabrication faster, the vertical joints seem to take place across a pane of glass or a panel. When this condition is compounded by the situation

Figure 10-4 The completed building using a curtain wall system. *Courtesy: Arcadia*

wherein the verticals are run through two, and sometimes three, stories in height, we are again talking about a sizeable amount of movement that no gasket or wet seal can take care of. Such expansion will chew up the system to the point where it will leak in any situation when subjected to noticeable amounts of water. An overwhelming number of the stick systems used in high-rise buildings do leak. As far as we are concerned, the only value a stick system has is that it is inexpensive. All too often, what the architects will get for their money when using such prefabricated systems that are field erected is less than expected.

It is of interest to note that the development of these metal stick systems occur in the design of storefronts, where they can be most successfully used. It is important to remember that the typical storefront is a low-exposure situation, one story, and usually protected by other architectural elements. When the same basic system is applied to a high-rise condition with high exposure, it just won't work. In theory it works, but in actuality its performance is highly questionable when used in any high-exposure area. Even storefronts in high-exposure situations will leak extensively.

Unitized Panel System

The other metal wall system is the unitized panel system, which was the traditional and original approach to achieve a weather-tight building. It is a system in which the panels are fabricated in a shop under controlled conditions. They are normally fabricated for one-story heights but can be two floors in size. They can be constructed to the width of any desirable scale or module, although they are somewhat limited to sizes that can be shipped by practical means.

The advantages of the panel system are many, including the fact that the joints can be designed to move without tearing the system apart. The edge conditions can be designed as an interlocking system where it is possible to obtain good sealant characteristics. It is even possible, through design, to control the location of movement to meet the architect's requirements rather than being a slave to the system. Internal joints can be welded or properly fastened so that they don't move. The entire system is a tighter situation and operation where the joints are not overstressed or crushed to the point of incurring water infiltration. Because it is a more expensive system, many designers shy away from its use and don't like to specify it. However, performance-wise, it is a well-known fact that the unitized panel system operates significantly better than the stick system. It is our position that the unitized panel system is the only curtain wall system to use in midrise and high-rise buildings.

FASTENINGS AND JOINERY OF METAL AND GLASS CURTAIN WALL SYSTEMS

The fastening of metal work is extremely critical to water infiltration–resistant design. Normally, the two systems used include:

- The screw spline method
- The shear block method

Associated with the screw spline method is the characteristic of being solidly connected using screwed joints. Screws are particularly good to use as fastenings of metal wall systems as long as they have full penetration. It is necessary that the screws go completely through the metal in a perpendicular relationship. A self-tapping screw, properly used, has tremendous holding capacity. Typically, this method requires that the vertical mullion be constructed from two pieces (split mullion) to allow the fabricator to access the screws fastening the horizontal mullions to the vertical mullion. The horizontal mullion extrusion includes C-shaped or half-circle splines that run parallel with the length of the mullion inside the tube and typically located near the four corners of the section. Sealant is then applied to the contact edges at both ends of the horizontal, at which point the horizontal is positioned and attached to the vertical mullion by screwing through the half section of the vertical mullion and threading through the splines of the horizontal. This method is typically used in unitized panel curtain wall systems.

The concern with the screw spline method is that it is subject to damage when self-tapping screws are not inserted into partial circle-shaped extrusions (screw splines) inline or parallel with the spline. What happens in this is that when the self-tapping screw goes down the spline in a crooked manner, the screw will tend to enlarge the spline to the point where much of the holding power of the screen is lost or, in fact, a good portion of the screw will pop out the open side of the spline. This can lead to having only a 10 to 15 percent bite of the screw threads to the walls of the spline. Situations have been seen where there is little, if any, holding power left and it is possible to pop out aluminum jamb members with a slight kick or a simple wrench of the hand on members fastened to the sill piece. By slight redesign or modification of the system used, it is possible to obtain complete penetration by the screw in order to guarantee a good grip or substantial hold on the members.

The shear block method, used in stick systems, involves fastening and extruded aluminum "shear block" to the vertical mullions with screws. The sections of the shear blocks vary from one manufacturer to the other; however, the principle is the same. Some are fastened to the vertical mullion through the back wall of the shear block extrusion, while other extrusions have splines through which the screw is threaded and bites into and through the side wall of the vertical. Once in place, sealant is applied to the contact surfaces of the shear block and the horizontal mullion section is then slipped over or "rocked" onto the shear block. The horizontal is then secured to the shear block by screwing through pre-drilled holes in the mullion and tapping into the wall of the shear block or into splines that are part of the shear block extrusion. Again, this is a very basic and simplified description of the assembly, and more detailed installation procedures are dependent on the curtain wall manufacturer written instructions.

Because the assembly methods vary, it is recommended that the architect request in the specifications for the submittals of the manufacturer's written installation instructions along with the shop drawings. As one can derive from the preceding discussion, both of the assemblies, screw spline and shear block, rely heavily on the use of sealant at the joints to prevent water infiltration; therefore, sealant capability testing should also be asked for in the specifications.

ANCHORING CURTAIN WALL TO STRUCTURE

Anchorage of the curtain wall to the building structure drives a lot of decisions in how the system is designed and installed. The types of anchors used are vast in shape, configuration, and size, but when all is said and done they all need to perform the same tasks. They must be designed to accommodate the combination of building tolerances and the tolerances within the curtain wall system itself. Clearances must be designed into the anchoring to allow for movement caused by temperature, seismic, and wind events. Lastly, the anchors need to be able to withstand and transfer dead loads, wind loads, lateral loads, and miscellaneous loading (i.e., building maintenance staging light shelves and sunshades to name a few). Anchors fall into two basic categories:

1. Gravity anchors or dead load anchors, as they are also known, are designed to resist the dead loads of the curtain wall and transmit it to the building structure. These connections are fixed and rigid and will resist all other loads acting on them as well, such as wind loads and lateral loads. Typically, in stick systems the vertical mullion will have one gravity anchor per section of mullion. Placement and spacing of these anchors are dependent on mullion design considerations.

2. Wind load/lateral anchors are designed to restrain the out-of-plane movement caused by wind acting on the curtain wall in either a positive or negative manner, while allowing lateral movement and/or vertical movement. Unlike gravity anchors that have standard bolt holes, wind load anchors have slotted holes running in the direction of the movement they are designed to accommodate. These anchors are located at points where gravity anchors are not. An example would be if anchoring a vertical mullion that spans two floors, a gravity anchor may be placed at the midpoint and wind load anchors place at the top and bottom.

Anchors are either bolted or welded (Figure 10-5 and 10-6) to the structure or, in the case of concrete structures, embedded in the concrete. The mullions are then through bolted to the anchors.

Bolted connections are solid and safe, but they are seldom designed for appropriate cross bearing of the metal members themselves. When a stainless steel bolt,

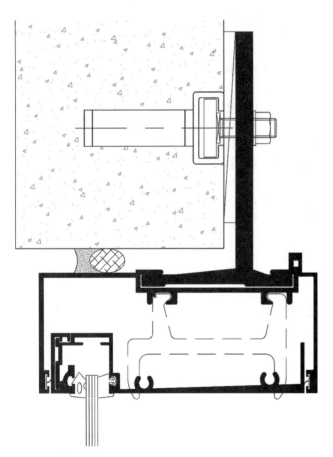

Figure 10-5 A curtain wall head condition bolted to structure. *Courtesy: Arcadia*

which has a high impact resistance, is used in a ⅛-inch-thick walled aluminum section, the forces acting on the aluminum can be immense and lead to a loose, moving situation when the aluminum yields to high stresses. To improve on this situation, fasteners through the mullion are sleeved. High-strength bolts are excellent for tensile situations but have no additional advantages when used on metals subject to cross bearing. Aluminum fasteners are not recommended for anchoring curtain wall systems. Ferrous metals should be avoided at all costs as fasteners at the mullion-to-anchor connection. They will result in all kinds of problems because of galvanic action. We recommend series 300 nonmagnetic stainless steel for exposed fasteners, but be aware of the critical aspects of each system.

Welding also produces a good solid connection but should be limited to the connections of the anchors to the embeds in the structure. Problems can arise if adequate precautions are not taken; there is a tendency to have "burn-throughs" or "gas pockets" and discoloration of the

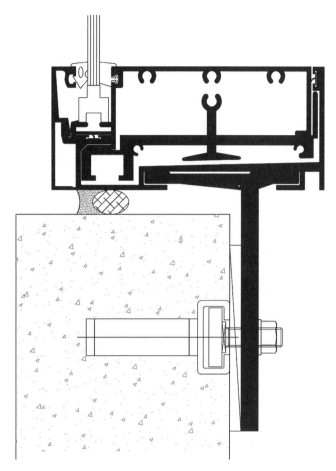

Figure 10-6 A curtain wall sill condition bolted to structure. *Courtesy: Arcadia*

metal, which is completely unacceptable where appearances are critical. Another problem that is consistently overlooked is the overheating aspects of welded connections. Aluminum loses its temper quality around the 800°F range, and can result in a localized loss of strength. This is particularly critical where structural welded connections are used to hold the aluminum wall system in place. For example, one system we have seen used steel clip angles to connect the aluminum wall system to the structural steel frame of the building. In the process of welding the clip angles to the structural frame, the clips became hot enough to overheat the aluminum where it was bolted to the clip angle. A localized strength loss resulted, which became critical because it jeopardized the integrity of the system designed to hold the entire wall system in place.

GREEN NOTE

Light and shade shelves are quite common in sustainable designed projects. These shelves are used to reflect natural sunlight deeper into interior spaces in order to supplement or replace artificial illumination. The shelves can be integrated or separate from the window assembly. Because these are horizontal projections, they exert torque on the building face and need to be addressed structurally and with regard to water infiltration. Architects need to pay particular attention when these shelves are part of the window assembly. These assemblies typically involve the use of structural steel inserted into the window mullions to support the shelves. In these cases, there is a heightened degree of potential

Light shelf and shade shelf projections reflect daylight into the interior of buildings, providing luminance in lieu of artificial lighting, but also create additional loads on window assemblies. *Courtesy: C. Kaneshiro*

failure due to the additional forces (torque, gravity, and uplift) placed on the window assembly, which could result in water infiltration. In this situation, we recommend that both shelves and window assembly be provided from a single manufacturer. In our experience, this avoids many of the problems that come from multiple manufacturers, including coordination of fabrication, installation, and water infiltration liability.

THE STRUCTURAL INTEGRITY OF THE WALL SYSTEM ITSELF

In addition to properly designed connections attached to the building, the wall itself must maintain its own structural integrity. Accordingly, the wall and its components must be designed with the capacity to resist wind, seismic, thermal, and dead loads.

In dealing with wind loads, again it is imperative that the architect allow for positive and negative pressures on the wall system. Concern for the negative pressures, which are usually considerably greater than positive pressures imposed on the wall, should govern the analysis of loads. It is extremely important to remember that the most weather-reported wind loads occur at the 30-foot elevation point. These published loads are universally inadequate for high-rise construction. In addition, the architect should not forget that unbalanced loads can take place within a single panel and can act in both a horizontal and vertical direction. In this regard, cantilever systems are most vulnerable to these unbalanced loads. Once the wall systems work loose or spring their joints due to the fact that they are incapable of resisting the unbalanced loads, significant leaks can and do occur. It is worth remembering that glass almost always blows out. It very seldom blows in.

Additional loading on the wall system will be generated by the building itself during extreme wind conditions. The building will sway from floor to floor, and the resulting action will impose critical loads on the wall, which also must be resisted without tearing the wall system apart.

Seismic loads on the wall system, though also applied laterally, are completely different in character than wind pressures. Loads resulting from an earthquake affect the entire building and all the wall systems on each façade of the building rather than producing positive and negative pressures on specific faces. Seismic loads can be transmitted directly to the wall system itself or may be imposed on the wall system by the performance of the entire building acting under the ground-shaking action produced by the earthquake. Floor-to-floor deflections of the building resulting from earthquake forces will impose considerable stress onto the exterior wall system and reduce its potential to resist water infiltration. Any wall systems that are attached to cantilevered structural systems are extremely vulnerable due to the cantilever's extreme vertical movement under seismic action. Floor-to-floor wall systems with rigidly fixed connections can be literally torn apart by the significant movement of the building during an earthquake.

The actual mass of the wall system itself is most critical when dealing with seismic forces. Generally speaking, the heavier the mass of the wall system, the greater the stresses produced by the acceleration effects of the earthquake. The building may not collapse under earthquake-imposed forces, yet damage to the wall system can still be severe. Again, continuous movement produced by the shaking of the wall itself will be enough to open up joints and result in evident water infiltration unless necessary design precautions are taken from the very start.

There is no way the architect can stop thermal expansion of wall systems. The available and reasonable fastening capabilities of metal wall systems on the market are often insufficient to do the job. The wall system will tear itself apart. This is particularly true for the stick system–type wall assemblies. The wall must be designed with its own structural integrity with capacities to take thermal loads. It is safe to say that thermal stresses are the single most destructive force of exterior metal wall systems. For example, a building 100 feet long subjected to normal 200°F variation will have a total expansion of the wall system used to clad the building's exterior. Thermal expansion movements must be accommodated to avoid severe water infiltration problems.

The wall system itself must be designed to take its own load. This is particularly true for the currently popular tall, all-glass buildings using up to 1-inch or thicker glass sections, which in themselves are extremely heavy. The wall system must be able to take the resultant loads with a comfortable safety factor applied for additional insurance. It must be able to resist such loads with very nominal deflections, or problems with the integrity of the glass will result. It must be remembered that these thick glasses have fairly large tolerance limits. The wall system must be able to handle the described loads and those thick glass tolerances adequately and comfortably. Under such circumstances, if a fairly thin, tenuous edge grip occurs at a critical point, problems will occur.

TOLERANCES

Construction tolerances come into play significantly in the installation and design of curtain wall systems. There are the fabrication tolerances within the curtain wall system itself as well as the building frame tolerances, which affect the installation of the system. The architect should keep in mind that the building tolerances set by the industry are considered ideal but are very seldom obtained in "realistic" conditions. One should also consider that many designs call for different building systems interfacing with one another and that these systems tolerances may be very different from one to the next. When designing the curtain wall and its attachment, the design professional should take into account the realistic tolerances and ensure that there is some sort of "quality control" program in place where the building tolerances can be monitored and brought back if they begin to encroach set limits throughout the construction of the building.

Suffice to say that in designing for realistic tolerances, construction conditions should be assumed at their worst. In the exterior wall design of the Pacific Design Center, dubbed "the Blue Whale," in Los Angeles, each floor has a plus or minus of 1.25 inch vertical movement and plus or minus 1.5 inch horizontal movement, under seismic action. The exterior glass wall system was detailed to take such variations without loss of integrity. Even with such extended tolerances, the wall system wasn't that much more difficult to design and make water resistant. Such building movements have been experienced in the Pacific Design Center, as the building is known to have gone through at least two sizeable earthquakes since its completion.

GLASS

When dealing with glass, the architect should know that all types of glass have tolerances that often are not met. It helps if the glass frame allows for full tolerance and then some. The size of the glazing pocket and amount of bite on the glass become crucial factors in the curtain wall design, especially where thermal and building movement are concerned. Because aluminum and glass have coefficients of expansion, the design professional can somewhat predict what the differential in expansion and contraction of the two materials will be based on the locale's changes in temperature and can easily design for such movement. If not designed for, the glass can incur stress by being bound between mullions, which can cause buckling of the glass or, in the case of thermal contraction in cold weather, the glass "walking" out of the glazing pocket and resulting in no bite on the glass or failure in the gaskets or seals. For movements between the building and the wall, the degree of movement becomes less predictable, and this is why the building tolerances become so important.

Several types of glass commonly used in curtain walls are:

- Sealed insulating glass, sometimes treated with low-emissivity coatings for energy concerns (Figures 10-7 and 10-8).

- Laminated glass, commonly used where safety glazing or impact resistance is required (Figure 10-9).

- Laminated insulating glass, which is a combination of the preceding two types.

Figure 10-7 A clear sealed insulating glass assembly used in a curtain wall. *Courtesy: H. Pajo*

Figure 10-8 A spandrel sealed insulating glass assembly used in a curtain wall. *Courtesy: H. Pajo*

■ Monolithic float glass, widely used where energy concerns or impact resistance are not issues.

■ Sealed insulating glass is a makeup of two or more glass lites separated by a steel or aluminum spacer (typically) and entirely sealed around its perimeter, enclosing air or an inert gas between the lites. The spacer typically contains desiccant that absorbs any moisture in the entrapped air in the airspace. Sealed insulating glass has special problems associated with it, with which the architect should be aware. One is that it has a high expansion rate, which could cause severe problems unless it is taken into account. Another problem related to this high expansion rate is that insulating glass sometimes cannot tolerate sharp shadow cutoff in full sun exposure situations. We are aware of one building that had full-time glaziers on hand just to replace the broken glass resulting from this condition.

It must be emphasized that sealed insulating glass has a tendency to be beset with problems, which in many cases can be described as a bad situation. First, there are all kinds of prices on the product, and the life span of differential products is very carefully defined. Some of the glasses are designed with a life expectancy of as little as two years. In one particular case involving a residence that utilized double-pane insulated glass, the inside cavity was full of moisture condensation after a two-year period, which completely obliterated the magnificent view toward which the house was oriented. Upon protest by the owners to the glass manufacturer, it was pointed out that the manufacturer's specifications of the glass clearly spelled out the two-year limitations on its use. Nothing could be done about it. Unfortunately, the owners were an elderly retired couple who could not afford replacement costs. It always behooves the architect to know what the limitations are in dealing with sealed insulating glass.

■ Laminated glass consists of two or more plies of glass with an interlayer of polyvinyl butyral (PVB) or cured resin sandwiched between each ply. PVB comes in a variety of thicknesses

Figure 10-9 A laminated glass assembly used in a curtain wall. *Courtesy: H. Pajo*

and formulations that need to be carefully specified based on the glazing applications. For example, if the glass is to be installed in a project that is located in a wind-borne debris region of the country, the codes may require that glass to meet certain impact resistances. This glass will require that the PVB layer be formulated for hurricane resistance at a thickness of 0.06 inch to meet a small missile impact rating. PVB is commonly used for most window applications; however, there are several other types of interlayers used, for example, aliphatic polyurethane sheets and resin-cured interlayers, typically polyester, urethane, or acrylic based.

Optical distortion either through the laminated glass or in the reflected image off the glass can be a relevant concern that may need to be address in specifying laminated glass. The distortion is caused by the roller waves that are inherent in heat-treated glass. This distortion becomes compounded when the two plies are laminated together, especially if the roller waves in each ply are offset from one another.

■ Laminated insulating glass, as mentioned before, is a combination of the first two types, consisting of a laminated lite with a metal spacer separating it from either another laminated lite or a monolithic lite, creating an air space between the two lites and sealing it around the entire perimeter. This type of glass is used when the design calls for both the benefits of laminated glass, whether it is impact resistance or acoustics, and the high thermal insulating characteristics.

A basic principal when working with any type of glass is to deal with a single manufacturer, carefully articulate your needs, have the manufacturer indicate what they can do to approach them, and get everything in writing. In addition, it is imperative to have samples of the glass that are marked and identified for job use. The architect should then stick to specifying that particular manufacturer "cold" without substitution. If allowances must be made for competitive bids, indicate what other manufacturers will be considered as alternates. They must come forth with a complete redesign of the system, satisfying all criteria that their glass has, and in no way should a straight substitution be allowed to take place.

It is obvious that for many of the esoteric glasses, the manufacturers do not have all the answers yet. Accordingly, let the manufacturers, rather than the architect, take the risk. In all opaque glass, it is important to control color variation and to insist on uniform coating thicknesses. Clear everything with the manufacturer and come to a complete understanding before the job starts because it will be too late to do anything about it later. Do not field cut special glass—ever! Such a practice will often lead to the glass's cracking.

Any glass product is far from standard. For anything unusual, clearly cover all conditions in the specifications and be prepared to hold the line. Federal Specifications DD-G-451c indicates and gives the many variations allowed. Read it through first and then make a decision in realistic terms.

GLAZING CONDITIONS

In glazing, one of the important considerations that warrants attention is the edge condition. There are many variations, including, among others, cut, polished, seamed, and rounded. If it is assessed to be a critical aspect of the glazing assembly, then it must be specified. If it isn't, then the architect should be prepared to accept most edge conditions delivered to the job site.

Another consideration is the edge grip condition, also known as "bite" (Figure 10-10), which requires considerable thought before detailing because different situations hold true for the type of glass to be used. The Glass Association of North America (GANA) has recommended minimum bite dimensions for both monolithic and insulating glass. In the use of monolithic glass, starting with ¼-inch-thick float, the edge bite should be specified and detailed as ⅜ inch minimum. It should be increased with the use of thicker glasses and grow to ¾ inch for 1-inch-thick glass. For insulating glass, ½-inch to 1-inch-thick units require an minimum of ½ inch;

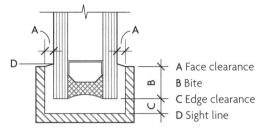

Figure 10-10 Glazing method terminology. *Courtesy: H. Pajo*

A Face clearance
B Bite
C Edge clearance
D Sight line

however, in a wind-borne debris region, the impact requirements may call for a ⅝- to 9/16-inch bite. When dealing with insulated glass, applied pressure on the glass should never exceed the manufacturer's recommendations or severe damage can occur.

When setting the glass in the sill pocket of the frame, two setting blocks made from either neoprene, ethylene propylene diene monomer (EPDM), or silicone should be used. They should have a durometer hardness of 85 plus or minus 5. Typically, the setting blocks are placed at quarter points of the sill and may be moved equally toward the corners; however, they should be held back from the corners a minimum of 6 inches. It is also important to edge block the glass; otherwise, the glass may "walk out" over a short period of time. The edge block should have a hardness as recommended by the glass manufacture generally having a durometer Shore A hardness between 50 and 70.

There are several methods of glazing, each having its advantages and disadvantages, but for this book we will discuss three of the most commonly used. The first method is known as the wet glazing, where either gun-grade sealant or preformed tape that is elastomeric material extruded into a long continuous ribbon is used as the primary seal between the metal frame and the glass on both the exterior and interior side of the glass lite. Silicone is typically used for this application. The architect must take care in specifying a sealant that is compatible with all the materials it will come in contact with, including the setting blocks, the material used to seal the insulating glass unit, or the interlayer material if laminated glass is used, and/or having provisions in the specification that call for compatibility tests to be submitted from the sealant manufacturer for all those materials. When the preformed tapes are used, it is recommended that gun-grade sealant be used at the corners of the unit to ensure a positive seal. This method, when done properly, is considered to be the most effective way of sealing the glass against water and air infiltration. The disadvantage is that it is labor intensive and relies completely on the quality of workmanship.

The second method is dry glazing, which uses premolded, extruded gaskets that are compressed between the metal frame and the glass to create the seal. One system uses a pressure plate, which is a continuous metal plate to which the low-durometer, closed-cell exterior compression gaskets are affixed. The glass panels are installed up against interior compression gaskets, and the exterior gaskets are compressed by screwing the pressure plate to the mullion. By torquing down the pressure plate to the manufacturer's recommended specification, a positive seal is achieved. Because there are joints at the corners of the gaskets, it is recommended that toe beads made with wet sealant be applied as a secondary line of defense to prevent leakage at those areas that are susceptible to water infiltration. When installing the toe beads, care must be taken not to plug any weep holes that may occur in the glazing channel. This system requires that the glass be installed from the exterior. The other system allows the glass to be installed from the interior. The exterior gaskets, again soft closed-cell gaskets, are affixed to a fixed glazing channel that is part of the mullion. The glass is set into the glazing channel, after which applied glazing stops that snap into the mullion are put into place. This is followed by rolling in a dense wedge-type gasket that applies force to compress the gasket, creating the seal. Wet sealant heel beads may be necessary to improve on the watertightness at the corners where gasket joints occur. Dry glazing systems are popular because of their speed and ease of installation. These systems also make compatibility and high quality of workmanship less of an issue.

The third method is structural seal glazing, which is used when a clean, smooth glass appearance is called for on the exterior of the building. The system works by adhering the glass to the metal mullion behind the glass with structural silicone sealant. The space between the two panes of glass is sealed with a weather seal. In some cases, the structural sealant will also act as the weather seal. This gives the appearance of a butt-glazed system from the exterior but should not be confused with such a system. Butt-glazed systems don't have mullion supports at the free edges of glass. There are two-sided and four-sided structurally glazed systems where the former is structurally glazed on two sides and conventionally glazed on the other two sides and the latter is structurally glazed on all sides.

If at all possible, try to glaze from the interior. It will save money in meeting the new Occupational Safety and Health Administration (OSHA) requirements that have raised the costs of buildings considerably within the past few years. Again, make glazing the responsibility of one contractor and avoid the situation of having several responsible parties getting into the act. It is considered good practice to make the wall system manufacturer responsible for glazing in order to avoid complications later.

11

Sealants and Gaskets

Exterior wall systems are only as good as their weakest element as far as water and air infiltration are concerned, and in most systems this is typically the joints, whether they be expansion, control joints, or joints at interfaces with other systems or materials. The weather-tightness of these joints relies heavily on the quality of the sealant or gasket material used to fill these joints and their installation.

SEALANTS

Sealants are one of the most rapidly changing products on the market due to recent advances made to their technology; manufacturers are constantly coming up with variations in most products. Silicones have had considerable upgrading in recent years, and as such are clearly the sealant of choices for glass and aluminum work. Unfortunately, they are not so good for wood.

There are many types of sealants that can be used effectively in water infiltration–resistant design. Rather than attempting to cover all of them, which would be beyond the scope of this chapter, only the general, generic capabilities of sealants will be presented. For each typical characteristic, special conditions exist that are known to be different. Basically, the architect has gun-grade, knife-grade, and flow-grade sealants to deal with. Flow grades can be partial leveling and self-leveling, and when self-leveling is indicated, the manufacturer *really* means self-leveling!

One job in Texas used a self-leveling material to correct some wind deficiencies. Someone had omitted a #10 screw during the erection of the wall system on the 14th floor of the building. A big, bulk loading gun was being used to fill certain sections of the wall system with this self-leveling material and no one had noticed that the particular screw was missing on the 14th floor.

At a critical point, one of the workers suddenly approached the supervising architect and indicated that a gun-and-a-half had been used at a specific point and it still wasn't full. Much to his horror, the supervising architect could only suspect the worst condition. He stuck his face against the glass and peered inside the building to see if the sealant had penetrated the interior and ruined the carpet or other expensive finish materials. When nothing was seen, he then cautiously leaned over the side of the scaffolding on the exterior of the building and saw a rich, deep rust brown stain running down the outside of the building for about 12 stories across glass, aluminum, spandrels, and everything else. What an unholy mess that turned out to be! It took more time to clean the self-leveling sealant off the side of the building than to complete the entire water infiltration correction job. The only effective way to remove it from the glass and metal was to allow it to harden or set and then scrape it off gingerly by hand.

Most sealant material, silicones excluded, have limitations when exposed to ultraviolet (UV) rays, which are very detrimental to them. One of the first problems known to us occurred on a building in San Francisco, where the entire building had to be reglazed. What happened there was the adhesive bond was completely destroyed by exposure to UV rays, which burned the sealant. This meant that when the sealant was used on the inside of the glass, the UV rays came through the glass and attacked the adhesive plane of the sealant. If the sealant had been used on the outside of the glass, the UV rays would still come through the glass and a portion of the UV would reflect off the inside face of the glass and attack the sealant again just as effectively as the interior glazing. Granted, it is a slow process, but it does happen and has happened several times over the life span of several buildings.

Now, most manufacturers have a coating they will furnish to apply to the glass that will act as a protective device. It is strongly urged that the protective coating be called for in order for better performance to be achieved. Most of these protective coatings are clear and will not produce a discoloring effect. It is still necessary to be careful with their use because most of them will turn a very slight milky white color after about a six months' exposure to UV rays. When this happens, it is next to impossible to get it off; it can't be scraped or dissolved off.

If the sealant failure is an adhesive one, it is almost impossible to find, and if found, it is almost impossible to get the joint cleaned again to protect it from further deterioration. This is the reason why most sealant beads are designed so that the adhesive plane is a much larger cross-section than the center of the bead. It also explains why it is necessary to put a backing rod in so that the joint can be tooled to neck down that area of cohesive characteristic. It is desirable in many ways to have the adhesive area, if possible, somewhere in the neighborhood of twice the width of the cohesive area.

Sealants are made to move. They work on a percentage of their original dimension. If a bead is an inch wide and it allows for a 25 percent movement, it means that the joint can go down to ¾ of an inch in size or up to a 1¼ inch without failure. But if a fillet bead is involved, or a sealant bead is put between two pieces of metal that are touching, even a millimeter of separation will induce an infinite amount of movement (Figure 11-1). No sealant can take that type of movement. Once the sealant starts to fail, it tends to have a zipper-type action. For this reason, most remedial work is insufficient when a tube of sealant is simply used to throw fillet beads all over the place such as corners and connections. Within a couple of years many of the failures will have reappeared.

In terms of the economics of sealants, cost considerations arise as a real consideration, but this is one area where it does not pay to use cheaper grades. The performance of the sealant, invariably, is almost a direct ratio to the cost of the sealant. Some sealants that have been used in water infiltration remedial work can cost $80 to $90 a gallon. Under the circumstances, this turned out to be the least expensive approach to the problem in the long run. However, if someone had used material that had cost $30 a gallon instead of $15 a gallon initially, in all probability the failure would not have occurred.

There are many types of sealant compositions. There are one-part materials,

Figure 11-1 Failed fillet bead; loss of adhesion is likely due to the expansive movement of the metal flashing. *Courtesy: P. Cuccia*

two-part materials, three-part materials, and under certain conditions it is possible to need four-part materials. One-part materials are mostly moisture cured, but a few are air cured. It is important to know which type of material is being used. The moisture-cured materials generally cure faster than the air cured. If they are to be applied in a very arid area, they should not be used because they will cure slowly. Special situations under certain circumstances have been resolved by sprinkling the material with a garden waterhose. It is not generally recommended, but it can be done. The problem with most of the one-part materials, whether they be moisture or air cured, is that they cure from the outside in. In doing so, there is a tendency to set up planes of cure. If it is a high-frequency moving joint, the movement during the cure cycle can set up fracture planes within the sealant areas and cause potential failure planes within five to seven years. In such cases, it is not common for cohesive failures to be set up and occur.

Most multipart materials are made with chemical cures so that they cure more uniformly through the mass of the sealant. They are of a much better grade sealant in terms of overall performance. Their problem, however, is that they require field mixing, which brings in problems of control. If they are factory mixed, they have to be stored in a frozen condition, which raises the price.

In working with chemically cured products, it is very critical to the application process that the manufacturer's recommendations be followed in the strictest sense. When the manufacturer's instructions indicate that the product should be mixed for a specific length of time, those instructions must be followed. Any deviation from the recommended time periods can produce negative results.

In one case, one of the authors was using an esoteric type sealant, called PR-40-MC, which was especially formulated to solve a very sophisticated water infiltration problem needs. Accordingly, that author, being so knowledgeable, didn't feel that it was necessary to read the instructions, which related to the mixing of this "wonder" material. Mixing instructions on the label of the can required that the contents be mixed at a speed of 125 revolutions per minute (rpm). As it turned out, the author did not have a drill readily available with the capacity to turn at such a slow speed. So a regular ¼-inch drill was used with a speed of about 1,200 rpm. Holding the can between his knees, he placed the mixing drill into the mixture and hit the switch for about two minutes, only to jump back and drop the drill when extreme heat hit his knees. He thought there was an electrical short, so he promptly unplugged the drill. He then reached down to pull the drill's mixing blade out of the can and found that it couldn't be done, the chemical mix had already cured and everything was a frozen solid mass. It was evident that the sealant had such a high thixotrophic characteristic that the high mixing speed created a high molecular friction. This raised the material's temperature enough to burn the knees of the author and "kick over" the curing properties of the mixture immediately.

All sealants become hard with age regardless of the manufacturer's claims. Test data presented by the manufacturers and government data should not be taken at face value. Most tests are based on data collected within a 7- to 30-day test period and under the most controlled conditions using brand new sample materials. In terms of practical field conditions, the data may be irrelevant.

General observation and comments presented on the characteristics of specific sealants are based on products within a given line of expected performance. They do not include remarks on cheap sealant or on some of the "junk" sealants that are on the market. The architect should never try to save money on sealants—it just isn't worth it. It is also important not to use form release materials, and best to avoid using sealants on exposed aggregate materials, both may lead to trouble later.

Acrylic Sealants

The first of these deals with acrylic sealants, which are not elastomeric to start with, despite general understanding to the contrary. Acrylics operate on a plastic flow base. Acrylics are unique in some aspects. They have very good adhesion initially and will even adhere to a dirty surface at the very beginning. In fact, it is even possible to lay a bead down under water and pour the water off, and adhesion will be obtained. They have no recovery and therefore should not be used in a moving joint situation. In a moving joint, when separation occurs, fresh material is exposed to the atmosphere, due to its plastic flow characteristics. When it comes together as the joint closes,

---

GREEN NOTE

Sustainable design encourages the use of materials that contain low volatile organic compounds (VOCs). These criteria basically measure the amount of toxic chemicals off-gassed by the product. The primary concern is with products that are used on the building interior (sealants, adhesives, carpets, wood laminates) and thereby reduce the indoor environmental quality and subsequently health of the building occupants. However, there should be an awareness of the VOC properties for exterior products as well, especially when such products are used in exterior courtyards, entries, and other locations where people gather. Exterior products, which off-gas VOC at very high levels for long periods of time, can be found in sealants, coatings, and adhesives. Use of these products in areas of assembly or concentration of occupants could create unhealthy environments, which would be counter to the intent of a sustainable building and also a liability concern.

instead of recovery, the sealant starts folding into itself. It keeps repeating this process of folding in, in, and in. After a few hundred cycles, depending on the size of the joint, this continuous action may cause the fold to go all the way through the sealant and probably constitute a flaw plane through the bead.

Another limitation of acrylics is what is called a reversion characteristic. It literally turns into a liquid and flows away under long-term water exposure. Acrylics do not have resistance to ozone or UV exposure and often turn into a substance that is as hard as a rock. In this regard, acrylics have poor life spans and thus can be classified as one of the poorer-grade sealant on the market. They probably should be called caulking.

Butyl sealants are also not elastomeric. They are plastic flow materials with little recovery. They have the same characteristics and limitations as acrylics with regard to UV and ozone exposure. However, butyls are very good sealants to use with wood as long as it is under compression and covered. Additionally, as is well known, butyl tapes are excellent for glass conditions. Unfortunately, when exposed to sunlight, butyls have a poor life span, even though they are tolerant of dirt. They also dry hard when exposed.

Polysulfide Sealants

Polysulfide sealants were the original elastomeric sealants. They have good to excellent elasticity, fair to good adhesion, and excellent cohesion. Polysulfides are still made in a wide range of products available. Ultraviolet and ozone cause some hardening and reduce the elastomeric properties. They are submersible, but do require a well-cleaned surface prior to application. They often require priming for adhesion, particularly when used with wood or concrete. Where used in straight adhesion, they only have about 10 to 15 percent elasticity, but they adhere to anything and everything, and it is next to impossible to remove them once applied. However, in warm and moist climates they have a record of losing their adhesion to glass. There are other polysulfides that have 30 to 40 percent elastic expansion properties but may not have good adhesion. It is necessary to determine what properties the sealants should have to fit the specific problem. All in all, polysulfides are an excellent material.

Polysulfides have a direct cost-versus-benefit ratio. They are obtainable in gun grade or a self-leveling class. They are subject to UV burn as described earlier, and therefore must be concealed or protected from the sun's rays.

Urethane Sealants

Urethanes have the widest range of sealant compositions available, and the widest variation in terms of quality. There are more poor-quality sealants available in urethane products on the market than most architects realize. The problem is that anyone with two garbage cans and an egg-beater can make urethane sealants. Quality variation is extremely wide. Generally speaking, for the price range, the good urethane sealants are the best general sealants on the market. They have an excellent life span; some are submersible, others are not, but all require extremely clean conditions for application. They do have limitations when subjected to UV burn on glass but much less so than the polysulfides.

The urethanes in general have a good, long life period and most should easily maintain their characteristic of 25 percent elasticity. They will not take a compression set, and are available in gun grade and self-leveling. They are currently the most common construction sealant in today's market.

Silicone Sealants

Silicones have probably made the greatest advancement in performance in recent years. They represent one of the best materials available on the market. They are the most stable sealant made and are not affected by UV or ozone exposure. A good silicone bead laid down correctly and carefully will last indefinitely with very little deterioration. However, it is as touchy as can be, and therefore is not always considered to be a good field installation material. Silicones are also notorious for attracting dirt, especially the lighter colors, and are very difficult if not impossible to clean.

The newer silicone products on the market are much better than the older ones. There have been many recent breakthroughs where adhesive problems with no workmanship tolerances have been much improved. It is our opinion that silicone is the best choice for aluminum and glass conditions. Silicone sealants are available in three modulus ratings: high, medium, and low. Each modulus sealant type is geared toward particular types of anticipated joint movement. High-modulus silicones are the hardest of the three and are used in joints requiring 25 percent movement in either direction. The low-modulus sealant has the greatest elasticity and is used in joints expected to expand up to 100 percent their construction width and contract to 50 percent. Low-modulus sealants are often used in joints for precast concrete panels, exterior insulation and finish system (EIFSs), and as perimeter sealants for curtain wall systems, just to name a few. To ensure proper adhesion, primers are typically required for most substrates when applying silicone sealants. One should confer with the sealant manufacturers on the type of primer required for the type of materials the sealant will be applied to.

Medium- and low-modulus silicones will skin over in 20 and 60 minutes, respectively, and take about 24 hours to as much as 4 days to fully cure, depending on the climate and the size of the joint. High-modulus sealants set up and cure rapidly, generally skinning over within 5 minutes of application—which leaves little time for tooling, so the applicator must move quickly—and fully cure in 12 hours.

As a general precaution when using any kind of sealant, if their conditions of use are in any way unusual, it is extremely important to contact the manufacturer and clarify all aspects of the application, including asking questions as to whether the intended use is in any conflict with their prescribed use. This should provide specifics of what can be expected as far as performance is concerned. It is best to obtain a written statement from the manufacturer so that it is all on record for future reference. If an ambivalent answer is received, it may be best to look for an alternate material. The architect or design professional should also include in his or her specifications the requirement for sealant compatibility testing to ensure that the sealant will adhere to the substrates and materials to which they are applied. As a second check to the compatibility tests, it is recommended to also include in the specification direction to perform field sealant pull tests, especially where sealants require primers to aid in their adhesion.

Sealant Accessories

Backup Materials

Backer rods are used in joints to be sealed and perform several tasks. These tasks include controlling the depth of the sealant; giving the back of the sealant proper shape; and supporting the sealant before, during, and after curing. Backer rods are made from a variety of materials, but the three most commonly used are the closed-cell polyethylene type, the open-cell extruded polyolefin type, and the semiclosed cell type. Closed-cell rods (Figures 11-2, 11-3, and 11-4) resist water penetration, keeping the back of the sealant dry; however, outgassing from a punctured backer rod can cause bubbles to form in the sealant, which in time can penetrate entirely through the material and breach the joint. Open-cell rods eliminate the problems arising from outgassing, but in the long term can absorb moisture and become saturated, which can cause failure in the sealant. The third type, the semi-closed cell, also referred to as soft-type backer rod, claims to solve the problems of the previous two types of rods. Picking the right type of backer rod often depends on the type of sealant used, the size of the joint, the type of joint, and the climatic conditions being dealt with. All in all, it is strongly recommended that the design professional talk with the sealant manufacturer as to what the best choice is.

Figure 11-2 Section of a closed-cell backer rod. *Courtesy: H. Pajo*

Bond-Breaking Material

In order for sealant joints to work properly, they need to be bonded to only the two sides of the joint. The terminated ends and the backs of the sealant need to be allowed to move freely. Bond breakers are introduced to control what the sealant does and does not adhere to. An example of where they are used is a perimeter joint around a door frame. For the most part, the gap will be backed with a backer rod, which the sealant will not adhere to, but the rod is often interrupted by shims, which should not be bonded to the sealant. A bond-breaker tape would be applied to the shim to prevent the adhesion and allow the sealant to move freely.

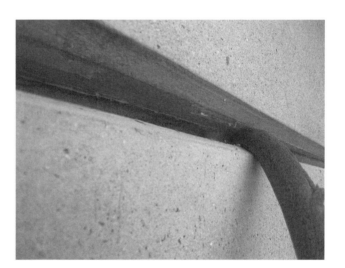

Figure 11-3 Closed-cell backer rod being installed prior to sealant application. *Courtesy: R. Inouye*

In pursuing workmanship standards, the cleanliness of the substrate and location of the application cannot be overstressed. It is extremely important to clean, clean, and clean again. There is only one way to clean properly—with white, dry, clean cotton rags. If the rags used are colored, the solvents used in the sealant may pick up the dye and contaminate the surface. If the rag is synthetic rather than cotton, no dirt will be picked up and removed. All that will happen is that the dirt will be smeared around.

Figure 11-4 A completed sealant joint between two precast panels.
Courtesy: R. Inouye

If the rag is not dry-cleaned, chances are that the solvents in the sealant will probably pull out the washing detergent's residue in the rag and contaminate the surfaces. The rag should not be dipped into a bucket of solvent, but rather the cleaner should be poured on the rag. Otherwise, all you will end up with is a contaminated bucket full of cleaner that will have to be discarded. Only small rags should be used, and in the final cleaning, the rag should be used only once and then thrown out. If the job is particularly difficult, it sometimes is appropriate to use "gun patches" simply because they are difficult to reuse.

There are several types of cleaners available. There are only a few cleaners that should be used in critical situations. The best is methyl ethyl ketone (MEK). It is highly flammable and must be used correctly. It should not be used in enclosed areas that are not properly ventilated, or a severe explosion can take place. It is also toxic and should not be touched or exposed to skin, as it will be absorbed into the body through the skin. Many mechanics ignore the toxicity and work with the liquid with bare hands. It has been noticed that after continuous exposure to the compound, one becomes extremely allergic to it. After repeated exposures, it can cause a most severe itching that will not disappear for several days. Attention should be paid to Material Safety Data Sheet (MSDS) standards. Unfortunately, MEK is currently illegal in many areas. This has forced the use of various substitutions. Some work; some do not. Triclonal ethylene is not flammable and is the only product that should be used if the job is in closed, unventilated spaces. However, it should never be used in a well-type operation because it is heavier than air. It is generated from a chlorine base, which can kill the worker if inhaling takes place. It is also slower in drying than the others and just a little more difficult to work with. Emphasis must also be placed on how dangerous this cleaner is.

When it comes to the installation of sealants, it is preferred to use air-pressure guns for consistency and uniformity. There are some experienced workers who prefer to use a handgun and do so quite successfully. In some cases it is difficult to tell the two types of installations apart when the handgun application is done by a true expert. The gun should always be drawn, not shoved, in order to avoid stringing the material out. Joints must be tooled. If someone states that they don't have to be tooled, that is a misstatement and should not be followed. A clean, dry tool should be used, as it improves adhesion and creates the proper shape and eliminates air pockets.

If frozen material is to be used, it is imperative that instructions are followed and the pot life carefully watched. Otherwise, it may start to prematurely cure and negate the positive characteristics of the sealant. Using sealants from a pot that has started to "kick over" is a waste of time.

GASKETS

Gaskets typically used in glazing applications, as well as sealing joints of exterior wall panels, are constructed from either closed-cell neoprene foam or dense neoprene or ethylene propylene diene monomer (EPDM). The dense gaskets are used in applications as described in Chapter 10, having a hardness ranging from 40 to 90 Shore A. The closed-cell neoprene gaskets also used in applications in the previous chapter tend to be softer and more compressive. Generally speaking, the best performance is achieved with neoprene gaskets (Figure 11-5), which have a 25 to 35 percent compression factor. It is recommended that architects attempt to obtain products for their project that have this characteristic. Anything less than the 25 to 30 percent compression may not handle appreciable movement adequately and may not be watertight under most conditions. Any product that has a compression factor over 40 percent has a tendency to take on a compression set, and the positive elasticity characteristics of the neoprene will be lost. Neoprene does tend to harden under exposure to solar radiation and may deteriorate over a period of time under such exposure.

Extreme care must be taken with the intersections that will probably occur on the job. When used in conjunction with a concrete panel, large chunks of the material are used, and it is not possible to deal with an overlap operation as is done normally with butyl tapes. Intersections and joints must be sealed with some care in order to

Figure 11-5 Profile of neoprene gaskets used to secure glazing come in various shapes. *Courtesy: H. Pajo*

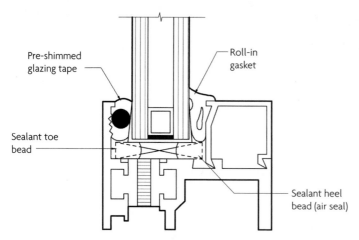

Figure 11-6 Toe, heel, and cap beads are used as a second layer of defense against water infiltration. *Courtesy: H. Pajo*

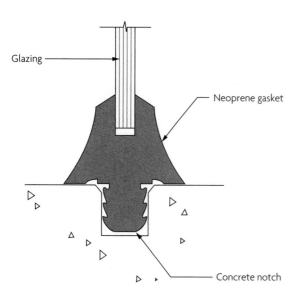

Figure 11-7 Structural gasket with spline that wedges into the concrete groove. *Courtesy: H. Pajo*

avoid later failures. Any good neoprene adhesive should be adequate, and once the gasket is in place the normal compression developed will keep the joint tight and under control. As a secondary line of defense in glazing applications, toe, heel, and cap beads can be used to reinforce corner laps and joints against water and air infiltration (Figure 11-6).

Another neoprene-type gasket in use in glazing applications is the preformed type, also known as structural gaskets (Figure 11-7). There are several variations to this type of gasket, such as those that set into a reglet, lap over a nib, lap over aluminum flanges, and other similar conditions. Almost all of them are zipper types or wedging types. Most are extruded solid material and are very dense, having a hardness of 75 ± 5 Shore A. They have the consistency of a rubber inner tube. We prefer the zipper type because it has a good homogeneous quality and very good structural integrity and is not subject to any kind of movement in the glass. One of the key factors of the zipper types is that it is difficult to install the glass into them at the corners. As such, it takes considerable effort to do it properly.

When the gasket is set, it is important that it is well set. Special tools must be used to install the locking strip so that the seam is uniform and consistent. If this is not done, installation problems will develop when a moment force that is not designed for is put into the gasket.

It is recommended that the zipper- or wedge-type gasket should never be used in concrete work without using a sealant in conjunction with the connection. The gasket material is not flexible enough to conform to the minute variations encountered in a concrete surface, including a steel-troweled surface.

The wedge type is a fairly new style of gasket and basically has an "L"-shaped configuration into which the glass is set prior to driving home an interlocking wedge to complete the installation. To date, their track record has been quite good when properly installed.

In both types of the gaskets described here, there is very little tolerance in the placing of the glass. It must fit. If the glass is oversized, it will have a detrimental action on the neoprene; if undersized, it will place excessive forces on the lip edge of the gasket, which was not designed to take such forces.

It is suggested that weeps be used on the inserts. When done in conjunction with a concrete wall, it costs more money and nobody likes it, but it does add a very good safety factor to the design. Most jobs cannot afford to have the type of picture frame installation that uses vinyl inserts, and therefore end up using single strips, which have weak intersection points when water gets into them. A properly installed gasket has outstanding performance characteristics. When correctly done, they will produce excellent results in water infiltration–resistant design. Personal experience has indicated that a quality gasket system tested under six inches of static head of water will give a satisfactory performance under any normal loading conditions seen at the job site.

BUTYL TAPES

Butyl tapes are an excellent material for small glazing systems. Many architects, including the authors, do not like them for large glazing systems because, after personal experience in their use, it has been found that they will not handle the movement of glass adequately. Another drawback of a butyl system is that once it has been installed for any time period, it is impossible to remove the glass for replacement purposes without breaking the glass.

Reinforced butyl is also an excellent material. Its properties will stop the pumping action and give some resiliency when used in pressure glazing or snap-in systems.

All gaskets must be installed under compression. They do not work unless they have a compression action that places them under stress. All gaskets, including butyl types, have problems at the intersections, and this must be watched carefully during installation. To the best knowledge available, preformed picture frame systems in butyl are not available, and consequently the corner intersections become critical in most installations. It has been noted that an overlap of about $\frac{1}{16}$ inch to $\frac{1}{8}$ inch at the intersections does an excellent job in sealing and does not create a large thickness of material, which normally causes the immediate and adjacent points to lack compression. This can cause localized infiltration.

As can be determined from this chapter, there is a wide variety of sealants and gaskets used to seal joints in walls and around perimeters of spandrel panels and glass. Design professionals must learn and understand the properties of the types of sealants and/or gaskets they want to use and determine whether they are the proper choice for the climatic and site conditions for the project. As has been repeated several times throughout this chapter, consult the sealant or gasket manufacturer to help select the appropriate type for the job.

12
Testing

In mid- and high-rise buildings, as well as some complex low-rise buildings, it is strongly recommended that full scale mock-up testing be done for the exterior wall systems, including *all* components that make up that wall system and all the interfaces as well. The architect needs to make sure that provisions are added to the specification to include such testing early on so as to be priced. The architect should also strongly encourage the owner or client not to put the testing portion of the project on the value engineering chopping block because the information gleaned from the testing is invaluable to how the "real" building will perform. In the long run, the testing will actually save money by finding out what the problems are before the actual construction begins as opposed to having to correct failures after the actual building well under construction.

In one major high-rise project, one of the authors' work on the façade testing was in place in the contract documents but came up as a potential value engineering item that the client was seriously considering. With the support of the curtain wall consultant hired by the client, the architect was able to save the testing from being cut, and it was a good thing, too. The mock-up testing revealed quite a few errors in the assembly of the components of the wall system including a serious failure of the window installation, all of which were resolved, recorded, and incorporated into the methods of installation for the actual building. Needless to say, the client was extremely relieved and appreciative that we talked them out of cutting the testing from the project.

For the same project, while the need for the mock-up was being discussed, the window manufacturer, whose window failed during the testing, was protesting about having to have their window included in the test because they had already run tests on their systems and had certificates proving they had passed the requirement for structural, water, and air. This may be and is typically the case for many manufacturers, but one must realize that the tests to get those certificates are performed in spotless laboratories where the windows are meticulously assembled, installed, and sealed by and under the strict supervision of the manufacturer's engineers—a far cry from how they are installed in reality. So the point we are trying to make is to "stick to your guns" when it comes to having mock-up testing for your project.

In testing, the single most important consideration is to understand that American Society for Testing and Materials (ASTM), American Aluminum Manufacturers Association (AAMA), and most industry standards represent the bare minimum for testing the quality of water infiltration–resistant systems. The building architect must thoroughly understand the exposure of the given location, establish performance criteria with the owner that will meet the given exposure, and then set a standard of performance that will satisfy the defined criteria. Any corresponding test should therefore always meet the performance criteria established and specified. Obviously, it will not do any good to specify a 3-inch static head condition only to have a ½-inch static head test performed. This will not produce realistic and accountable results.

The specifications should call for the testing mock-up to be constructed and tested at a certified testing facility as well as for the submittal of shop drawings and material for the mock-up. The contractors who were awarded the bid to do the work for the project and their subcontractors must be the ones to construct the mock-up using the methods, procedures, materials, and tools they will use for the actual building. Testing of the mock-up should be performed, the data analyzed and retested if warranted by the results, and approved before submitting the shop drawings for the "real" building and definitely prior to the extruding of any metal.

Any mock-up fabricated is not an absolute or a guarantee, but rather it represents only an indication to the architect where the potential weaknesses are in the proposed wall. So it is important to have the mock-up done early before anything is solidified. It is impossible to get a manufacturer to change anything after 50,000 pounds of metal have been extruded—it just won't be done. Anyone who thinks that a manufacturer will set up an entire system of dies to run sample extrusions without extra fees is simply kidding themselves. The set-up charge for an extrusion process is expensive, so the manufacturer will go ahead and punch out the whole operation with the intention of later attempting to convince the building design to accepting the system as a solution by using the materials already prepared. Under such conditions, it is not viable to run any objective tests prior to the fabrication of any preconceived solutions.

THE MOCK-UP

In taking the mock-up itself under consideration, it is absolutely stupid to have a complex wall design and then turn around and perform the test on a simple, flat panel. The mock-up should cover all major conditions and critical components of the wall, with particular attention to corners and joints. Corners, overhangs, reentrant angles, or whatever is designed as part of the total wall system must be reflected accurately in the mock-up to be tested. Make sure that expansion joints and any other unusual conditions are covered.

When the mock-up is built, make sure that it is constructed to the maximum allowable tolerances that will be found on the job. It is useless to build a mock-up with jewel-like precision under controlled manufacturer's conditions when it is known that such exacting conditions will not exist on the job. Anyone can make a model work with chewing gum plugging all the critical areas for testing purposes, so it is incumbent on the architect to impress on the manufacturer that it is a learning experience for both rather than a test of wills. If any defects or weak points are to be revealed, it is best that they occur during the testing cycles rather than after the building has been occupied. For best results, we believe it necessary that the architect should actually watch the erection of the wall mock-up for testing. If the testing process includes people or testing technicians who come out in spotless white coats, the architect should be suspicious and must be prepared to say, "Forget it." Testing staff, on the other hand, with dirty fingernails and greasy overalls is an indication that a realistic and objective test will be conducted without overly fastidious conditions that will not be duplicated on the job site later.

The architect should supervise the actual testing process. The dumbest thing that can occur is for the architect to arrange for a testing laboratory to conduct the necessary tests and then sit back and wait for the receipt of an 8½-by-11-inch sheet of paper that lists the results. Under such situations, the outcome is inevitable—no one would have learned a single thing by failing to observe the actual test and see how the weak points perform or fail to perform. When there is failure it should be analyzed to see what the cause is and rectify it and test it again.

THERMAL EXPANSION TEST

Prior to testing for thermal expansion, the mock-up should be tested for water and air filtration and succeed to establishing that the wall system is indeed working correctly. This sets a basis so as to determine later if there is a failure caused by the thermal testing. The test is performed by enclosing the exterior side of the mock-up within an insulated chamber. This chamber contains equipment that enables the test personnel to control the ambient temperature range of the air. The temperature range is specified based on the climatic conditions the wall is expected to endure. The limits should exceed anything that can be reasonably expected on the job site by at least 50 percent. The test begins at a specified indoor temperature, and during the first hour the temperature is brought up to the highest temperature of the specified range. For the next two hours this temperature is maintained. In the fourth hour, the temperature it is brought back down to the starting temperature, only to continue in the next hour to the lowest temperature in the range, and is held at that temperature for two hours. Finally, within the last hour of the cycle, the temperature is adjusted back up to the starting temperature. The total duration of a cycle is a minimum of eight hours. While AAMA 501.5 calls for a minimum of three cycles, we recommend that the architect settle for nothing less than a process that includes at least five cycles. In any case, the architect must never settle for test limits that are less than anything expected in reality. Following the thermal tests, the mock-up should be visibly inspected and allowed to stabilize at the ambient temperature for a minimum of six hours, possibility more, depending on the materials used for the wall system; concrete or masonry walls, for example, may take a longer time to stabilize. After the specimen is stabilized, it is recommended that a series of air and water infiltration tests be completed in order to see if the thermal cycling affected the performance of the wall system. In order to pass, there can be no signs of permanent damage or deformation, and the wall must meet the air and water infiltration requirements specified for the project.

SEISMIC MOVEMENT TESTING

The seismic tests should be carried out in two directions in order to realistically test and evaluate expected performance criteria. The test entails having the mock-up attached to the chamber's structural system, which represents the edges of the floors, that is able to maneuver and provide the amount of displacement specified for the test. This apparatus is connected to a series of hydraulic jacks, pistons, pulleys, or chain hoists that control the movement. The apparatus will rack the wall assembly for the specified displacement in one direction parallel to the wall face, then in the opposite direction to make up one cycle. This is repeated for three cycles. The wall is then racked for the specified displacement in one direction perpendicular to the wall face and then in the opposite direction to complete a cycle. This cycle is also repeated three times. Such a test will reveal whether the glass will fall out during lateral loading and if the necessary tolerance limits are met without putting any permanent deformation sets in the metal. Also, the joints designed for movement should be inspected to see that they move or slide freely without binding up. This can't be done without the architects actually being present during the test and in a position to get as close to the test assembly as possible during the seismic series in order to see all actions of movement encountered. Typically, a series of air and water infiltration tests are to be completed to check that the wall system's performance is retained.

AIR AND WATER INFILTRATION TESTS

During these series of tests, it is important that the architect be present inside the test chamber to watch for critical situations. If the chamber is a tall one, a stepladder should be used to inspect the mock-up system from all angles and heights. Start from the low point and work up to the highest point so that the entire wall system is covered. During this operation, it is important to tape all glass openings in the wall system so that if any failures occur, the glass will not shatter and severely cut or injure someone who is working close to the test specimen. Watch for water leakage and try to determine where it is coming from, the threshold of action taking place, and any other characteristics of the leakage. Try to run the tests at incremental levels of increase, and after they have been concluded, run a cycling operation with at least two cycles per minute from zero to whatever the maximum requirements are. When dynamic tests are being run, notice whether the cycles are setting up a pumping action, which will set up different patterns of infiltration in comparison to those that occurred during the static tests. In some projects it is recommended that the tests be kept running until leaks do occur even after the limits of the design criteria have been passed, in order to learn as much about the weak points of the system as possible for future reference.

Water Penetration Test under Dynamic Pressure

In this test, the mock-up has an air stream equivalent to the static differential air pressure specified for the project applied to it while water is sprayed over the entire mock-up at a rate of five gallons per hour per square foot for a period of 15 minutes. The air stream is supplied from a device, typically an aircraft propeller (Figure 12-1), capable of producing the air pressure specified for the test.

Figure 12-1 Modified aircraft engine and propeller used to apply wind pressure to the façade of the mock-up.
Courtesy: P. Cuccia

Figure 12-2 Spray towers used to evenly distribute water across the face of the mock-up. *Courtesy: P. Cuccia*

The water is supplied by a spray tower that consists of a series of pipes with series of spray nozzles and hoses that are distributed in such a way as to cover the entire face of the mock-up with an even dousing of water at the rate specified (Figure 12-2). The mock-up is considered to have passed if no water leakage is evident during the testing period. AAMA 501.1 defines water leakage as "any uncontrolled water that appears on any normally exposed interior surfaces, that is not drained back to the exterior, or that can cause damage to adjacent materials and finishes."

Air Infiltration Test (ASTM E 293)

The air infiltration test is performed in accordance to ASTM E 283. The test involves covering and sealing the mock-up completely with polyethylene sheeting, while leaving the chamber uncovered. A positive pressure differential of the specified value, typically 6.24 psf, is developed on the chamber by pulling air through the chamber. The airflow required to maintain this pressure is recorded and represents the base airflow value through the chamber. The sheeting is then removed from the mock-up, and the design pressure is reestablished. The airflow required to maintain the pressure is again recorded. The difference between the two recorded values becomes the airflow value through the mock-up. If this number is below the specified allowable rate of air leakage, then the mock-up passes; if above, then it needs to be determined where the point of failure is. This can be done by sealing around all windows and doors with the plastic sheeting and running the test again. If the airflow is within the allowable, wall joints and interfaces can be ruled and attention can be focused on the openings. To pinpoint which opening or openings are the culprit(s), the sheeting can be removed from each opening, one at time, and the test run for each opening. When one opening is found to be a leak point, it should be recorded and resealed and the test run for the rest of the openings in the same manner to determine if they may also be points of leakage. The method of sealing and testing the specimen will vary based on the design and configuration of the mock-up.

Water Penetration Test under Static Pressure (ASTM E 331)

This test is similar to the water penetration test under dynamic pressure with the exception of how the pressure is applied to the mock-up. The positive test pressure is established on the mock-up by pulling the air through the chamber until the specified pressure is reached and is maintained for the duration of the test, typically 15 minutes. The pressure established is 15 percent of the design load, so, for example, if the design load for the wall is 70 psf, the test pressure would be set to 10.5 psf. For high-performance wall systems, the testing pressure can be raised to 20 percent of the design pressure. When the test pressure is reached, the entire mock-up is then subjected to water on the entire exterior at a rate of five gallons per hour per square foot for the duration of the test. During the testing, the interior of the mock-up should be visually inspected for any water penetration. As with the dynamic testing, no water leakage is allowed in order for the mock-up to pass. If leakage does occur, it should be determined what the cause is, after which a plan of action should be established to remedy the problem, preferably while still at the testing site, so that the fix can be implemented and retested without delay.

Structural Test (ASTM E 330)

The structural tests are performed on the mock-up with pressure being applied in both the positive and negative directions, at incremental percentages of the design pressure. For example, the mock-up will be tested at 50, 75, 100, and 150 percent of the design pressure, also known as the test load. The tests are designed to observe the deflection in the wall and its components and whether any permanent deformation occurs. Using the preceding 70-psf design pressure example, the first part of the test procedure preloads the mock-up with 50 percent of the test load and then 100 percent of the test load as follows: The mock-up has a positive pressure of 35 psf applied to it and held for 10 seconds. The pressure is released, and the mock-up is allowed to recover for not less than one minute and not more than five minutes at zero load. Initial readings are taken and recorded by sensors placed throughout the testing chamber that will read the deflection in metal framing members, anchor deflection, and glass deflection. Pressure is then applied up to 70 psf and held for 10 seconds. The deflection readings are recorded during this holding period, and the pressure is reduced back down to zero. The test is then performed in the negative direction with the same load increments and hold and recovery times. Initial readings and deflection readings are taken at the same point of the test, as with the positive pressure test. In order to pass, no deflection of any metal framing members shall exceed L/175 of the clear span or ¾ inch, whichever is less. Anchor deflection in any direction shall not exceed $\frac{1}{16}$ inch, and glass deflection shall not exceed 1 inch.

These tests are performed again, only at the 75 percent and 150 percent increments, known as the proof load, in the same manner, for positive and negative pressure. For these tests, the acceptance criteria are as follows: There shall be no glass breakage or permanent damage to framing members, no permanent set of more than L/1000 is allowed, and no permanent set in anchors exceeding $\frac{1}{16}$ inch. The proof load is the test load multiplied by a factor of safety; in this case, the factor is 1.5 times the test load, which is typically what is called for by ASTM E 330.

The actual sequence of the testing process is very critical. When performing the thermal expansion test, it is important to conduct the water penetration and air infiltration tests before and after the thermal test, as discussed earlier in this chapter. In looking at the standard sequencing of the tests, you will notice that after the seismic and structural test a series of water penetration and air infiltration tests are done. This is an extremely important part of the testing in that it determines whether the deflection, movements, and stresses placed in the specimen during the structural and seismic test have any effect on the water and air performance of the wall. Following is the typical sequence of tests that may be ordered for a particular project:

- Preloading, where the mock-up is exposed to 50 percent of the design load in the positive direction
- Air infiltration test
- Water penetration test under static pressure
- Thermal expansion test
- Repeat air infiltration test
- Repeat water penetration test under static pressure
- Water penetration test under dynamic pressure
- Structural test at test load in positive and negative directions
- Repeat air infiltration test (optional)
- Repeat water penetration test under static pressure
- Repeat water penetration test under dynamic pressure
- Seismic movement test at design displacement
- Repeat air infiltration test (optional)
- Repeat water penetration test under static pressure
- Repeat water penetration test under dynamic pressure
- Structural test at proof load in positive and negative directions
- Repeat air infiltration test (optional)
- Repeat water penetration test under static pressure
- Repeat water penetration test under dynamic pressure
- Seismic movement test at $1.5 \times$ the design displacement
- Repeat air infiltration test (optional)
- Repeat water penetration test under static pressure
- Repeat water penetration test under dynamic pressure

Some series may call for a structural test to the point of failure for informational purposes only.

When all the tests have been completed, the assembly should be taken apart in the presence of the architect so that every individual piece of the wall assembly that comes out of the test chamber is critically examined, with particular attention paid to fastenings and other connections. Look for holes that have been subjected to extreme stress situations and forced "out of round," or bolts which that have been severely affected by sheear action. Any sign of water noted after the test should be taken as an indication of the potential of excessive problems occurring in the long haul or life span of the wall assembly system.

Finally, after all tests have been reviewed and evaluated, the architect should maintain a posture of not believing everything that is seen. Nothing should be taken for granted, and at all times the architect should be the harshest critic possible on every single point. The worst thing that can happen is for the architect to "fall in love" with his or her design and allow personal feelings to cloud the facts. The dollars at stake in large-scale design commissions are too great to allow judgment to be influenced by pride of design ownership. If there is any sign of failure during any parts of the testing sequence, it is best to bring it out into the open immediately and objectively evaluate the cause and effects.

GREEN NOTE

Sustainable projects also have potential testing criteria for certain aspects of performance mainly concerning indoor environmental quality. Some of the tests noted in the LEED for Building Design and Construction Guidelines V3.0 follow. We have noted the specific credit or prerequisite for which the test is referenced.

- Blower door test in accordance with ANSI/ASTM-E799-03 is used to measure the sealing of residential units for air leakage (LEED IAQ Prerequisite 2).

- EPA Compendium of Methods for the Determination of Air Pollutants in Indoor Air are step-by-step sampling and analysis procedures for evaluating pollutants in indoor air samples. This test is an option for testing indoor air quality prior to occupancy (LEED IAQ Credit 3.2).

- ANSI/ASHRAE 52.2-1999 Method of Testing General Ventilation Air-Cleaning Devices for Removal Efficiency by Particle Size is used to evaluate the filter media of heating, ventilation, and air conditioning (HVAC) systems (LEED IAQ Credit 5).

Take a careful look at any and all failures, determine if it can be corrected, see what the economic ramifications are, discuss it with the owner/client, and take steps to solve the defect in an objective way as soon as possible without blowing one's credibility by glossing over any potential problem. All recorded fixes to previous failures during the testing that have been retested and passed must be incorporated in the shop drawings and installation instructions for the construction of the actual wall system. This directive needs to be stipulated in the specifications of the mock-up testing, and the architect reviewing the shop drawing submittals needs to make sure that this has been incorporated; if they have not been, the submittal will be rejected and required to be resubmitted.

The testing does stop here, though; we recommend that in the specifications there be a requirement for fielding testing the wall assembly as

Figure 12-3 Field testing apparatus applied to a sliding glass door to test for air and water infiltration. *Courtesy: P. Cuccia*

the construction progresses. These field tests evaluate the water and air resistance of the wall at certain stages of completion throughout the building to ensure that the installation procedures and product quality are without problem or defect and are consistent. Areas selected to be tested need to have all components completely installed, adjusted clean, and sealed around perimeters and at joints. A test chamber that is typically constructed of plexiglass sheets, sealed and/or taped to wood framing, is applied and sealed over the area to be tested (Figure 12-3). A reversible blower or exhaust fan with a hose is sealed to the Plexiglas wall of the chamber to provide the airflow required to pressurize the chamber. The chamber is equipped with measuring devices to record airflow and pressure.

For the air infiltration test (ASTM E 783), the area to be tested on the opposite side of the chamber is sealed with polyethylene sheeting. The airflow is adjusted through the chamber to obtain the test pressure specified. When the pressure is reached and stabilized, the airflow is recorded as the base value of airflow. The sheeting is then removed and the test performed again, and when the pressure differential is reached, the airflow is recorded. The comparison of the two values are used in the same way as the air infiltration test done at the testing lab to quantify the amount of air leakage through the test area.

With the chamber still in place, a spray rig is set in place, having spray nozzles spaced out on a uniform grid (Figure 12-4) to begin the water penetration test (ASTM E 1105). The spray rig is calibrated to evenly apply water to the test area at a rate of five gallons per hour per square foot. With the water being applied at the prescribed rate, the airflow is adjusted once again to reach the design pressure differential across the test area and held for the 15-minute duration of the test. As with the laboratory test, no uncontrolled water penetration is allowed.

It is worth repeating that testing is extremely important to a project because of the time and money it actually saves in the long run, not to mention the effect it can have on the quality control of the wall system construction. Without it, the potential for failures, headaches, and financial implications are immense.

Figure 12-4 Field testing spray rig is set in place, having spray nozzles spaced out on a uniform grid. *Courtesy: P. Cuccia*

13

Installation

Proper installation procedures start by having proper specifications written.

Specifications are half of the construction documents of a project, with drawings being the other half. Since specifications take precedence over drawings in the case of conflict, one could argue that specifications are more important. Each specification section contains three parts:

Part I: General

Part II: Products

Part III: Execution

It should be noted that both Parts I and III have a significant impact on the installation of a product. Part I includes information on acceptable installers, testing, mock-ups, preinstallation meetings, and storage. Part III includes procedures for preparation, installation, cleaning, and protection of the installed product.

Since specifications become part of the construction contract, it is vital for the architect to make sure that these documents are written to include the appropriate procedures for installation of a product. If a specific test or preconstruction meeting (Figures 13-1 and 13-2) is not written in the specifications, then the contractor will have little motivation to comply without a change order.

Figure 13-1 A preconstruction meeting with the architect and contractor. *Courtesy: C. Kaneshiro*

Figure 13-2 View of a project in progress. *Courtesy: C. Kaneshiro*

It has been our experience that specifications are best written when the writer is an integral part of the design team. This allows the writer to understand the project requirements and conditions so as to produce a better document. Too often, we have seen specifications produced by aloof or isolated spec writers who do not understand the project at all or, worse, a project manager attempting to produce a specification by "pasting" together sections of old specs for a new project. Either case has the potential for disaster down the road.

Many young architects have little or no idea about the purpose of a specification. They seem to lack any training about the importance of this document. Most even don't know the basic organization of a specification. With so much focus in architectural education on digital drawing and the technologies that produce these drawings, basic instruction on this critical aspect of construction documentation appears to be missing. As such, it is crucial for architectural firms to provide continued education on this subject, especially when young architects are placed in project management, project architect or construction administration roles.

One might expect that for large commercial projects, a seasoned architect would serve as the construction administrator, but for smaller commercial projects there is typically not enough fee to assign a heavily experienced construction administrator. In such cases, younger architects are given this responsibility and asked to sink or swim. While small commercial projects carry less liability than large projects, the potential litigation from these projects can still have significant cost and time-consuming ramifications.

Manufacturers' guidelines provide the basis for most of the information needed in a specification. The architect should not veer from the manufacturer's directions. Alteration of the installation procedures may affect the performance of the product and could also impinge on the warranty. The architect and specification writer would also be wise to involve the manufacturer's representatives in the development of specifications, especially for products with complex installation procedures.

Complex assemblies or critical products such as below-grade waterproofing should consider including a preinstallation meeting to review the actual site conditions, materials, and procedures prior to installing the work. The architect, manufacturer's rep, general contractor, and subcontractors should be present. Be sure to record minutes for this meeting, as it would be helpful in the case of any future problems or litigation.

Over the years, we have noted a steady decline in the performance and capabilities of general contractors. This is not a testament of every contractor in the industry, and there are many contractors who provide excellent expertise and service. However, in general, project managers and engineers directing construction seem to have less experience and knowledge about construction methodologies. Part of the problem is the same market conditions that we have discussed as impacting architects

GREEN NOTE

As discussed in Chapter 3, commissioning is the process of testing, adjusting, verifying, and training to assist the design and construction team to deliver a facility that operates as a fully functional system as per the design intent. It has been our experience that the largest value in commissioning is during the installation and occupancy period. We have found great value in having an outside entity facilitate the implementation of important systems of a building. During construction, the contractor and his subs are generally focused on meeting the schedule and there is little time or inclination to provide adequate quality control. In one recent experience, the commissioning agent discovered during start-up that the mechanical subcontractor had installed the air handlers to the wrong condenser units. The units started up fine but would have reduced the life span of the units in the long term.

COMMISSIONING CHECKLIST
EXHAUST FAN PRESTART and START-UP CHECKLIST

PROJECT: _____			UNIT NO. _____				
LOCATION: _____			SERVICE: _____				
MANUFACTURE: _____			MODEL: _____				

ITEM	Commission Agent	Mech Sub	Elec Sub	Test/ Bal	Controls	Owner	CM
Prestart Inspection							
Equipment submittals reviewed							
Mounting checked w/shipping bolts removed							
Vibration isolators, seismic restraints, and guards installed							
Pulleys aligned and belt tension correct							
Plenums clear and free loose material							
Fans rotate freely							
Fans, motors, and linkages lubricated							
Fire and balance dampers positioned							
Electrical connection complete							
Disconnect switch installed							
Overload heaters in place (sized correctly)							
Fan room clean for start-up							

Example of a typical commissioning checklist. This one is for an exhaust fan unit. *Courtesy: C. Kaneshiro*

such as quickly evolving new products, specialization of the profession, and the demand for fast-track delivery methods. Furthermore, the construction industry seems to have more "project managers"—contractors who manage a plethora of subcontractors but do not perform any construction themselves.

The bottom line is that more than before, the construction personnel with direct influence on direction of the work seem to lack the knowledge and experience to ensure that products are installed properly. The architect should assess the capabilities of the contractor from an early stage of the project, and if it is determined that there is a lack of sufficient confidence, the architect should consider the following options:

1. Discuss with the contractor (sensitively) increasing the capabilities of their team.

2. Discuss the situation with the owner.

3. Increase vigilance on the installation procedures, preconstruction meetings, testing, and use of manufacturers' representatives to ensure the proper use of products.

That being said, one of the critical things about observation is that the architect should never be arrogant in the field. Time should be taken to explain the work to the workmen as to what is being called for and why. When a workman informs you that something doesn't look right, pay attention and always look very carefully at the situation described. If the workman is incorrect, tell him why he is wrong, and if he is correct, be sure to take steps to solve the problem or condition in a professional manner. In any event, be sure to thank the workman for calling the situation to your attention. Workmen who have complete confidence in your professional judgment and personal integrity will support everything that you are doing and can be your biggest booster in getting a wall system installed correctly with the highest standards in workmanship. However, they can make the architect look like an idiot and are prone to do so on the many occasions when the architect asks for it.

In terms of installation, it is important to recall that specifications should never be used to call for the impossible or to camouflage a difficult situation. Specifications should never be used as a bluff in the supervision of work because the experienced workman will simply call the architect's bluff when he realizes that the architect doesn't know a "hill of beans" about the given situation. In writing specifications on the installation of wall systems, try to visualize the problem from the workman's position and assign realistic tasks rather than attempting to minimize the problem. Workmen are just as human as you are and will respond to realistic challenges, but not impossible ones.

Also, it is important to take into account the location and exposure of the installation process. A true professional is also a human professional and one who has understanding when called for without compromising the situation. There is no substitute for being able to conduct oneself professionally but with understanding.

Tolerance limits must be observed realistically during the installation phases. If adjustments must be made, they must be realistic and fully explained to the owner/client before the fact rather than after, particularly if any trade-offs are called for. Everything should be approached with caution in critical areas, for in many cases the minutest of adjustments can cause the greatest problem later. Be aware of what is happening and on all counts, and never skimp on installation procedures. Be sure that they are followed as closely as possible at all times.

14
Conclusion and Summary

The key to all successful water infiltration–resistant design is for the architect to be competent and professional at all times, starting with a careful analysis of the forces that act on the design solution generated by building exposure and ending with the installation of the designed project, whether it be a roofing system, a wall system, or the smallest component, such as a gasket. Nothing should ever be taken for granted, and the impossible should always be interpreted as being in the realm of possibility when dealing with water infiltration.

The owner/client and workmen on the job must be treated with respect for their positions at all times. By explaining difficult situations to them prior to the time the situation becomes an insurmountable problem, it will be found that many serious misunderstandings can be avoided later. The mark of a true professional is one who has complete confidence in any action undertaken, but also one who is quick to see problems developing and solving them as soon as possible before they grow into big problems by getting out of hand. There is no substitute for quick, rational, and fair decisions on the job site.

Testing procedures should be supervised at all times. The architect who remains aloof and refuses to take part in the test by entering the test chamber is only asking for trouble later. An unsupervised test is no test at all and is completely worthless. A successful test is a learning process and not a test of wills between the design professional and the manufacturer or fabricator.

It is important that the design professional understand the limits of all products and assemblies used and not attempt to see that those limits are surpassed during design and/or installation phases. The purpose of a testing series is to confirm those limits in real-life terms so that adjustments can be made if need be prior to installation. Tolerance limits as well as test limits must also be understood. There are no substitutes for experience, and the faster a professional becomes acquainted with potential job site problems, the more understanding will be developed on all sides of the design/construction process to everyone's benefit.

Professional liability has reached a critical phase, reaching into all aspects of the construction process. Water infiltration–resistant design is but one issue that architects must face in realistic terms, along with a list of other concerns that is growing day by day. By being competent and professional at all times in rendering architectural services, the architect has won half the battle. A professional attitude must be borne at all times regardless of problems encountered and solutions proposed.

Have fun.

Bibliography

American Architectural Manufacturers Association (AAMA). *Aluminum Curtain Wall Design Guide Manual.* Schaumburg, IL: AAMA, 1996.

American Architectural Manufacturers Association (AAMA). *Glass and Glazing Guidelines.* Schaumburg, IL: AAMA, 1997.

American Architectural Manufacturers Association (AAMA). *Installation of Aluminum Curtain Walls Guidelines.* Schaumburg, IL: AAMA, 1989.

American Architectural Manufacturers Association (AAMA). *Joint Sealants.* Schaumburg, IL: AAMA, 1991.

American Society of Civil Engineers (ASCE). *ASCE 7-05 Minimum Design Loads for Buildings and Other Structures.* Reston, VA: ASCE, 2005.

Brantley, L. Reed, and Ruth T. Brantley. *Building Materials Technology: Structural Performance and Environmental Impact.* New York: McGraw-Hill, 1996.

Brock, Linda. *Designing the Exterior Wall: An Architectural Guide to the Vertical Envelope.* Hoboken, NJ: John Wiley & Sons, 2005.

Canada Mortgage and Housing Corporation. *Exterior Insulation and Finish Systems—Best Practice Guide: Building Technology.* Ottawa, ON: Canada Mortgage and Housing Corporation, 2004.

Canada Mortgage and Housing Corporation. *Glass and Metal Curtain Walls— Best Practice Guide: Building Technology.* Ottawa, ON: Canada Mortgage and Housing Corporation, 2004; reprinted 2005.

EIFS Industry Members Association (EIMA). *Guide to Exterior Insulation and Finish Systems Construction.* Morrow, GA: EIMA, 2007.

Fisette, Paul. "House Wrap vs. Felt." *Journal of Light Construction,* November 1998.

Glass Association of North America. *Glazing Manual, 2004 Edition.* Topeka, KS: Glass Association of North America, 2004.

Glass Association of North America. *Laminated Glazing Reference Manual, 2006 Edition.* Topeka, KS: Glass Association of North America, 2006.

Henshell, Justin. *The Manual of Below-Grade Waterproofing Systems.* Hoboken, NJ: John Wiley & Sons, 2000.

Kubal, Michael T. *Waterproofing the Building Envelope.* New York: McGraw-Hill, 1993.

Maylon, Gary J. *The Metal Lath Handbook: A Guide to Products and Installation, and Their Relationship to Portland Cement Stucco.* Trussville, AL: Metal Lath Consultants Co., LLC, 2002.

National Roofing Contractors Association (NRCA). *The NRCA Roofing and Waterproofing Manual,* 5th edition. Rosemont, IL: NRCA, 2003.

National Concrete Masonry Association (NCMA). Water Repellents for Concrete Masonry Walls (TEK 19-1). Herndon, Virgina. 2006.

Panek, Julian R., and John Philip Cook. *Construction Sealants and Adhesives,* 3rd edition. Hoboken, NJ: John Wiley & Sons, 1991.

Portland Cement Association (PCA). *Portland Cement Plaster/Stucco Manual.* Skokie, IL: PCA, 2003.

Sheet Metal and Air Conditioning Contractors' National Association (SMACNA). *Architectural Sheet Metal Manual,* 6th edition. Washington, DC: SMACNA, 2003.

Smith, Baird M. *Moisture Problems in Historic Masonry Walls: Diagnosis and Treatment.* Washington, DC: U.S. Dept. of Interior, National Park Service, Preservation Assistance Division, 1984.

U.S. Green Building Council. *New Construction and Major Renovation Reference Guide, Version 2.2,* 3rd edition. Washington, DC: U.S. Green Building Council, 2006.

U.S. Green Building Council. LEED Reference Guide for *Green Building Design and Construction, Version 3.0,* 2009 edition. Washington, DC: U.S. Green Building Council, 2009.

Glossary

Albedo

The proportion of the incident light that is reflected by a surface

Alkaline

Containing or having the properties of an alkali; having a pH greater than 7

Asphalt

A dark brown to black bitumen pitch that melts readily; a petroleum product

ASTM

American Society for Testing and Materials

Blister

An enclosed pocket of air, which may be mixed with water or solvent vapor trapped between impermeable layers of felt or membrane or between the membrane and substrate

BIM

Building information modeling

Bituminize

To treat with bitumen, a sticky mixture of hydrocarbons found in substances such as asphalt and tar

Built-up roof

A continuous, semi-flexible roof membrane, consisting of multiple plies of saturated felts, coated felts, fabrics or mats assembled in place with alternate layers of bitumen and surfaced with mineral aggregate, bituminous materials and liquid-applied or granule-surfaced cap sheet

CAD

Computer-aided drafting or design

Capillary action

The action by which the surface of a liquid, where it is in contact with a solid, is elevated or depressed, depending on the relative attraction of the molecules of the liquid for each other and for those of the solid

Cantilever

A projecting structure, such as a beam or floor plate, that is supported at one end and carries a load at the other end or along its length

Cavity wall

An exterior wall, usually of masonry, consisting of an outer and inner wythe separated by a continuous air space, but connected together by wire or sheet-metal tiles

Climatological

The general weather conditions prevailing in an area or region over a long period

Commissioning (building)

A quality assurance process during and following building construction which typically focuses on the mechanical and electrical systems

Condensation

The conversion of water vapor or other gas to liquid phase as the temperature drops

Conifer

Mostly needle-leaved or scale-leaved, cone-bearing gymnospermous trees or shrubs such as evergreens, pines, spruces, and firs

Counterflashing

Formed metal or elastomeric sheeting secured on or into wall, curb, pipe, rooftop unit, or other surface, to cover and protect the upper edge of a base flashing and its associated fasteners

Damp-proofing

A treatment of a surface or structure to resist or retard the passage of water

Daylighting

Design practice of placing windows or other openings such as skylights and reflective surfaces so that during the day natural light provides effective internal lighting replacing the use of artificial lumination

Deciduous

A tree or shrub that sheds its leaves annually

Dovetail

A fan-shaped tenon that forms a tight interlocking joint when fitted into a corresponding mortise

Elastomeric

A flexible substance occurring naturally, as natural rubber, or produced synthetically, as butyl rubber or neoprene

EPDM

Ethylene propylene diene monomer, a type of roofing membrane

Epoxy

Synthetic, thermosetting resins that produce hard, chemical-resistant coatings and adhesives

Extrusion

A fabrication process in which heated or unheated material is forced through a shaping orifice or die in one continuously formed film, sheet, rod, or tubing

Façade

The face of a building, especially the front or principal face

Felt

A fabric composed of matted, compressed fibers, usually manufactured from the cellulose fibers found in wood, paper, or rags or from asbestos or glass fibers

Ferrous

Of, related to, or containing iron

Fiber insulation board

Building material composed of wood fiber, cane, or other fiber material, compressed with a binder into sheet form

Flash butt welding

A technique for joining segments of metal rail or pipe in which segments aligned end to end are electronically charged, producing an electric arc that melts and welds the ends of the segments, yielding an exceptionally strong and smooth joint

Flashing

A thin, impervious material used in construction to prevent water penetration and/or to direct the flow of water, especially at roof details, between roof and wall and over exterior door openings and windows

Galvanize

Steel or iron coated with a protective layer of zinc

Hip

Inclined external angle formed by the intersection of two sloping roof planes

Hydraulic cement

A cement that is capable of setting and hardening under water, relying on the interaction of the water and the constituents of the cement

Hydrostatic pressure

The pressure equivalent to that exerted on a surface by a column of water of a given height

HVAC

Heating, ventilation, and air conditioning

In situ

In the original or natural position

Joint

A place or part at which two or more things are joined

Keene's cement

A hard, white, high-strength, quick-setting finishing plaster made by burning gypsum at a high temperature and grinding to a fine powder and adding alum; also known as gypsum cement

Lee side

The sheltered side; the side away from the wind

LEED

Leadership in Energy and Environmental Design, a building certification system for sustainable or "green" buildings administered by the United States Green Building Council

Microclimate

The climate of a small area or specific location in contrast with the climate of the entire area

Mineral capsheet

Roofing sheet coated with asphalt and surfaced with mineral granules

Modified bitumen roofing

Roofing consisting of composite sheets of a polymer-modified bitumen, often reinforced with various types of mats or films and sometimes surfaced with films, foils, or mineral granules

Plasticizer

A solvent added to a synthetic resin to promote plasticity and workability and to reduce brittleness

Schematic design

Part of the first phase of the architects' basic services in which the architect provides scalable drawings that show the relationship of the various program elements requested by the client typically including floor plans

Scrim

A coarse, meshed material such as wire, cloth, or fiberglass that spans and reinforces a joint over which plaster will be applied

Seismic

Of or related to an earth vibration typically caused by an earthquake

Self-tapping screw

A fastener that taps and drills its own hole during application

Sill

The bottom horizontal framing member of an opening such as below a window or door

Storefront

The side of a store or shop facing a street

Substrate

The surface upon which the roofing or waterproofing membrane is applied

Straw bale construction

A building method that uses bales of straw (commonly wheat, rice, rye, and oat straw) as structural elements, insulation, or both

Sustainability

A means of configuring civilization and human activity so that society, its members, and its economies are able to meet their needs and express their greatest potential in the present, while preserving biodiversity and natural ecosystems, planning and acting for the ability to maintain these ideals in the very long term

Terrain

A stretch of land, especially with regard to its physical features and topography

Thermal expansion

The change in dimension or volume of a material or body due to temperature variation

Thermoplastic

Material that is soft and pliable when heated, as some plastics, without any change of its inherent properties

TPO

Thermoplastic polyolefin, a type of roofing membrane

UL

Underwriters Laboratories, Inc.

Urbanization

To make urban (related to the city) in nature or character

Valley

Internal angle formed by the intersection of two sloping roof planes

Vapor barrier

A moisture-impervious layer of coating that prevents the passage of water or water vapor into a material or structure

Waterproofing

Treatment of a surface of structure to prevent the passage of water under hydrostatic pressure

Weep holes

Small openings whose purpose is to permit drainage of water that accumulates inside a building component

Appendix A: Unit Conversions

DIMENSION, AREA, VOLUME

1 in.	=	2.54 cm
1 ft.	=	0.3048 m
	=	30.48 cm
1 mile	=	1.609 km
1 ft²	=	0.0929 m²
10 ft²	≈	1 m²
1 ft³	=	28.32 L
1 m³	=	1,000 L
1 quart	=	0.94 L

The symbol "≈" means "equals about."

MASS, FORCE, DENSITY

1 lb m (mass)	=	453.6 g
1 kg	=	2.2 lb m
1 N	=	1 kg·m/s²
1 lb f (force)	=	4.45 N
1 lb	=	7,000 grains
1 lb/ft³ (density)	=	16 kg/m³

1 L of water has mass of 1 kg.

PRESSURE

1 Pa	=	1 N/m²
1 atm	=	29.921 in. Hg
	=	407 in. of water
	≈	3.3 ft. of water
	=	760 mmHg
	=	14.7 psi
	=	101,325 Pa
	=	101.325 kPa

$$= 1.01325 \text{ bar}$$

1 psi	=	6.9 kPa
1 in. water	=	248.84 Pa
	≈	250 Pa

(The symbol "≈" means "equals about.")

TEMPERATURE

°F	=	°C · 1.8 + 32
°C	=	(°F − 32) / 1.8
°R (absolute)	=	°F + 459.67
K (absolute)	=	°C + 273.15

WORK, HEAT, ENERGY

1 J	=	1 N · m
1 Btu	=	1.055 kJ
1 kWh	=	3.60 MJ
1 therm	=	12,000 Btu

POWER

1 Btu/h (Btuh)	=	0.2931 W
1 T, refrigeration	=	12,000 Btuh

RATE OF HEAT TRANSFER

$$1 \text{ Btu/hr-ft}^2 = 3.155 \text{ W/m}^2$$

THERMAL CONDUCTIVITY, K

$$1 \text{ Btu-in./hr-ft}^2\text{-°F} = 0.1442 \text{ W/(m · k)}$$
$$1 \text{ Btu/hr-ft-°F} = 1.731 \text{ W/(m · k)}$$

OVERALL HEAT TRANSFER COEFFICIENT, U

$$1 \text{ Btu/hr-ft}^2\text{-°F} = 5.678 \text{ W/m}^2 \cdot \text{K}$$

THERMAL RESISTANCE, R

$$1 \text{ ft}^2\text{-hr-°F/Btu} = 0.176 \text{ m}^2 \cdot \text{K/W}$$

PERMEABILITY

$$1 \text{ perm} = 1 \text{ grain/hr-ft}^2\text{-in. Hg}$$
$$1 \text{ perm} = 57.45 \text{ ng/h} \cdot \text{m}^2 \cdot \text{Pa}$$

ENGLISH / METRIC CONVERSIONS

English	Metric
1″	25.4 mm
1′	304.8 mm
1′	0.3048 m
1 psi (lb/in^2)	0.0068948 MN/m^2
1 ft^2	0.0929 m^2
1 lb/ft^3	16.019 kg/m^3
1 lb	0.454 kg
0.0394″	1 mm
39.37″	1 m
3.2808′	1 m
145.14 psi (lb/in^2)	1 MN/m^2
10.76 ft^2	1 m^2
0.0624 lb/ft^3	1 kg/m^3
2.205 lb	1 kg

Appendix B: Roofing Comparisons

LOW-SLOPE ROOFING

- Low-slope defined as $\leq$ 3:12 (25% slope, not less than .25:12, 2% slope).

- Includes built-up, modified bitumen, single ply (thermoplastic and thermo ply), sprayed polyurethane foam (SPF), and metal types of roofing.

BUILT-UP ROOFING

- Built-up membranes composed of alternating layers of bitumen (asphalt) and sheets called felts, usually four plies.

- A base sheet is either adhered or fastened mechanically to the substrate.

- Felts are fiberglass or polyester. Polyester has greater puncture and tear resistance, thus decreases chance of failure.

- Application methods include "hot-mopped" or "cold" applied. (Heat vs. solvents.)

- Exposed asphalt weathers quickly and either surfaced with aggregate or field-applied coatings like alum-pigmented asphalt, acrylic, reflective or nonreflective asphalt emulsion.

- Cap sheets may be applied, but not counted as a BUR system ply.

- Aggregate surfaces help, but blow off easily.

- Types I through IV, runny vs. stiff respectively. Type I penetrates better, Type IV is ideal for steeper roofs.

MODIFIED BITUMEN ROOFING

- Tough and handles abuse.
- Composed of prefabricated polymer-modified asphalt sheets.
- Polymers are added to the bitumen to enhance various properties of the bitumen.
- There are two primary types of modified bitumen roofing:
  - Atactic polypropylene (APP) plastic, heat-weld applied and uses base sheet, ply sheet(s), and cap sheet.
  - Styrene-butadiene-styrene (SBS) rubber, hot asphalt applied similar installation to APP roofing.

SINGLE-PLY ROOFING

- Thermoplastic membranes (single-ply) are flexible sheet materials that are used in one-ply or one-layer configurations as low-slope roof membranes.
- Thermoplastic roof membrane materials' chemical and physical characteristics allow them to repeatedly soften when heated and harden when cooled.
- Thermoplastic membranes:
  - Polyvinyl chloride (PVC)
  - Compound thermoplastics
  - Thermoplastic polyolefin (TPO)
- Thermoset membranes:
  - Ethylene propylene diene monomer (EPDM)
  - Chlorosulfonated polyethylene (CSPE)
  - Polyisobutylene (PIB)

POLYURETHANE SPRAY FOAM ROOFING (SPF)

- Constructed by mixing and spraying a two-component liquid that forms a base for an adhered roofing system.
- Primer is applied initially to aid in adhesion of the SPF.
- Expands 20 to 30 times in volume from its initial liquid state.
- Protective surfacing is required on the SPF. Elastomeric coatings with or without granules, and single-ply membranes are commonly used.

METAL ROOFING

- Not typically considered as a low-slope roofing (as low as ~QF″/ft.), but NRCA recommends at least ~HF″/ft. The greater the slope, the greater the leakage protection.
- Must be able to protect the entire area as a membrane.
- Steel or aluminum panels are used, specify Galvalume. Copper is available but seldom used.
- Two primary types of roof include:
  - Standing seam
  - Flat seamed architectural panels
- Structural Standing Seam
  - Resists water infiltration under hydrostatic pressure as a barrier.
  - Standing seams raise the joints above the waterline and sealed.
  - Panels are usually structural in nature to span purlins.
- Architectural Standing Seam
  - Architectural panels require a solid roof deck to support it.
  - Generally, panels are water-shedding (hydrokinetic) and may require steeper slopes.
- Flat Seam Metal Roofing
  - Flat seam roofing requires a solid substrate.
  - Material for this type of roofing is preferably copper.
  - All joints must be completely soldered to make the roof system completely weatherproof.

STEEP-SLOPE ROOFING

- Steep-slope defined as > 3:12 (25% slope).
- Includes metal, shingles and panels, asphalt shingles, tile, slate, and wood types of roofing.

METAL ROOFING

- The greater the slope, the greater the leakage protection.
- Must be able to protect the entire area as a membrane.
- Steel or aluminum panels are used, specify Galvalume. Copper is available but seldom used.
- Two primary types of roof include:
  - Standing seam
  - Flat seamed architectural panels
- Structural Standing Seam
  - Resists water infiltration under hydrostatic pressure as a barrier.
  - Standing seams raise the joints above the waterline and sealed.
  - Panels are usually structural in nature to span purlins.
- Architectural Standing Seam
  - Architectural panels require a solid roof deck to support it.
  - Generally, panels are water-shedding (hydrokinetic) and may require steeper slopes.
- Flat Seam Metal Roofing
  - Flat seam roofing requires a solid substrate.
  - Material for this type of roofing is preferably copper.
  - All joints must be completely soldered to make the roof system completely weatherproof.

METAL SHINGLES AND PANELS

- Metal shingles and panels are press-formed during the manufacturing process to provide a variety of shapes. These shapes emulate asphalt, tile, slate, or wood shingle configurations.
- They are interlocked or overlapped and directly fastened or clipped to the roof deck. Fasteners should be compatible with the metal roofing material to prevent galvanic corrosion. (Avoid dissimilar materials).
- Steel or aluminum panels are used, specify Galvalume. Copper is available but seldom used.
- Finishes include coatings of clear acrylic-based glazing, ceramic granules, or crushed stone chips.
- Installed on solid wood sheathing or wood furring.

ASPHALT SHINGLES

- Manufactured in the United States since the early 1900s.
- Newer products come in various colors, shapes, and patterns.
- Asphalt shingles are composed of asphalt, fillers, a reinforcing mat, and a granule surfacing. Granule surfacing is applied to reduce weathering and protect it from ultraviolet rays, increase fire resistance, provide colors and blends, and add weight for increased wind resistance.
- Considered as a multilayered water-shedding system relying on slope.
- Most shingles contain adhesive, self-sealing strips to secure the edge of subsequent layers of shingles.
- Underlayment configurations include: single-layer felt, single-layer polymer-modified bitumen, and double-layer felt.
- Generally installed over wood decks and attached with round-headed, sharp-pointed, corrosion-resistant roofing nails.

TILE ROOFING

- Many types of tile roofing, generally classified by shape and composition.
- Components of the roof tile include field, ridge, hip, and rake tiles that have various shape and function. Two major material types are clay and concrete:
  - *Clay:* Made primarily of high-quality clay and shale deposits. Materials are crushed and ground into a powder, wetted and formed by pressing or extrusion. Natural clay colors or glazes are applied to produce a wide variety of textures and colors.
  - *Concrete:* Composed of portland cement, water, and sand or fine aggregate, mixed and extruded under high pressure. Comes in different weights (per sf). Some tiles are compacted in molds to create the shapes. Color is applied by spraying pigments or glazes.
- Both are placed into kilns. Clay tiles are fired at high temperatures, while concrete tiles are dried.
- The tiles are usually allowed to cure before shipping, so that design strengths and physical properties may be achieved.
- Verify weight of roofing system lbs./sq. ft. to make sure the roof structure is adequate support.

SLATE ROOFING

- Slate is a type of rock that was created as hot lava flowed over clay deposits. This mixture eventually dried in layers, forming a hard rock that may be split into roofing material.
- Commercial slate is approximately ³⁄₁₆″ to ~QF″ thick and available in uniform sizes and shapes.
- There are several states in the United States that provide slate, and some are imported from Spain, China, South Africa, and other countries. Be sure that tiles are tested based on ASTM C 406, "Standard Specification for Roofing Slate."
- The layering properties of slate give natural cleavage planes. These planes allow slate to be easily split into thin layers. Slate also possesses a natural grain that is at right angles to the cleavage.
- Color of slate is determined by its chemical and mineral composition, and various shades of the same color may be used to create a blend.
- Verify weight of roofing system lbs./sq. ft. to make sure the roof structure is adequate support.

WOOD ROOFING

- Wood shakes and shingles are obtained by logging and sawn and split into individual units.
- Shakes have a rough and textured surface, while shingles' surface is sawn flat and smooth.
- Cedar and southern yellow pine wood species are used, but cypress, redwood, and oak also are used.
- Comes in three grades; no. 1, 2, and 3. No. 1 is best. No. 2 and 3 are used as starter or under coursing.
- Wood shakes and shingles may be pressure treated to preserve and give fire resistance to them.

Appendix C: Sealant Classifications

ASTM C 920

TYPES

Type	Description	Pros	Cons
Type S	Single component, typically air or moisture cured	Ease of use; no mixing, meaning less labor	Longer cure times, higher material expense
Type M	Two or more components chemically cured	Faster cure time and more consistent	Quality control concerns on the mixing of components; more labor intensive

GRADES

Grade	Description	Applications
Grade P	Pourable sealant, also referred to as self-leveling	Typically used for horizontal applications, sealants for traffic use are generally this grade
Grade NS	Nosag sealants	Used for traffic and nontraffic conditions, typically vertical joints and sloping horizontal joints

CLASSES

Class	Description	Applications
12-½	Sealant capable of handling movement, either contraction or expansion, of 12.5% of the original joint width	Nonmoving-type joints to joints with minimal movement
25	Sealant capable of handling movement, either contraction or expansion, of 25% of the original joint width	Joints designed for moderate amount of movement

Continued

Class	Description	Applications
35	Sealant capable of handling movement, either contraction or expansion, of 35% of the original joint width	Joints designed for moderate amount of movement
50	Sealant capable of handling movement, either contraction or expansion, of 50% of the original joint width	Joints designed for moderate amount of movement. Typically used in building façade systems and glazing
100/50	Sealant capable of handling movement of 50% contraction and 100% expansion	Joints designed for high amounts of movement; commonly used in façades of buildings in high-wind and/or seismic regions

USES

Use (Related to Exposure)	Description
Use T (Traffic)	Sealants used in joints subjected to vehicular or pedestrian traffic
Use NT (Nontraffic)	Used in horizontal joints not exposed to traffic, and for joints in walls, around fenestration, etc.
Use I (Immersible)	Sealants designed for use in areas subjected to water immersion
Use (Related to Material)	Description
Use M	Sealants used in contact with mortar
Use G	Sealants used in contact with glass
Use A	Sealants used in contact with aluminum
Use O	Sealants used in contact with all other materials other than those previously listed

Appendix D: Industry References

AA – Aluminum Association
1525 Wilson Boulevard
Arlington, VA 22209
http://www.aluminum.org

AAMA – American Architectural Manufacturers Association
1827 Walden Office Square, Suite 550
Schaumberg, IL 60173-4268
http://www.aamanet.org

ABAA – Air Barrier Association of America
1600 Boston-Providence Highway
Walpole, MA 02081
http://www.airbarrier.org

ACI – American Concrete Institute
P.O. Box 9094
Farmington Hills, MI 48333-9094
http://www.concrete.org

ANSI – American National Standards Institute
1819 L Street, NW, 6th Floor
Washington, DC 20036
http://www.ansi.org

ARMA – Asphalt Roofing Manufacturers Association
750 National Press Building
529 14th Street, NW
Washington, DC 20045
http://www.asphaltroofing.org

ASCE – American Society of Civil Engineers
1810 Alexander Bell Drive
Reston, VA 20191-4400
http://www.asce.org

ASHRAE – American Society of Heating, Refrigerating and
Air-Conditioning Engineers
1791 Tullie Circle, NE
Atlanta, GA 30329
http://www.ashrae.org

ASME – American Society of Mechanical Engineers
Three Park Avenue
New York, NY 10014-5990
http://www.asme.org

ASTM – American Society for Testing and Methods
100 Barr Harbor Drive
West Conshohocken, PA 19428-2959
http://www.astm.org

AWPA – American Wood Preservers Association
P.O. Box 361784
Birmingham, AL 35236-1784
http://www.awpa.com

CMHC – Canadian Mortgage and Housing Corporation
700 Montreal Road
Ottawa, Ontario
K1A 0P7
http://www.cmhc-schl.gc.ca

EIMA – EIFS Industry Members Association
513 West Broad Street, Suite 210
Falls Church, VA 22046-3257
http://www.eima.com

GANA – Glass Association of North America
2945 SW Wanamaker Drive, Suite A
Topeka, KS 66614-5321
http://www.glasswebsite.com

IMI – International Masonry Institute
42 East Street
Annapolis, MD 21401
http://www.imiweb.org

MRA – Metal Roofing Alliance
E. 4142 Highway 302
Belfair, WA 98528
http://www.metalroofing.com

NBEC – National Building Envelope Council
1090 Vermont Avenue, NW, Suite 700
Washington, DC 20005-4905
http://www.bec-natioanl.org

NCMA – National Concrete Masonry Association
13750 Sunrise Valley Drive
Herndon, VA 20171-4662
http://www.ncma.org

NIST – National Institute of Standards and Technologies
100 Bureau Drive, Stop 1070
Gaithersburg, MD 20899-1070
http://www.nist.gov

NGA – National Glass Association
8200 Greensboro Drive, Suite 302
McLean, VA 22102-3881
http://www.glass.org

NPCA – National Precast Concrete Association
10333 N. Meridian Street, Suite 272
Indianapolis, IN 46290
http://www.precastsolutions.org

NRCA – National Roofing Contractors Association
10255 W. Higgins Road, Suite 600
Rosemont, IL 60018-5607
http://www.nrca.net

PIMA – Polyisocyanurate Insulation Manufacturers Association
7315 Wisconsin Avenue, Suite 400E
Bethesda, MD 20814
http://www.pima.org

PCI – Precast/Prestressed Concrete Institute
209 W. Jackson Boulevard # 500
Chicago, IL 60606
http://www.pci.org

RCI – Roof Consultants Institute, Inc.
1500 Sunday Drive, Suite 204
Raleigh, NC 27607
http://www.rci-online.org

SMACNA – Sheet Metal and Air Conditioning Contractors National
Association
4201 Lafayette Center Drive
Chantilly, VA 20151-1219
http://www.smacna.org

SPRI – Single Ply Roofing Industry
411 Waverly Oaks Road, Suite 331B
Waltham, MA 02452
http://www.spri.org

Index